# Catholicism Revisited
## A Guide for the Perplexed

# Catholicism Revisited
## A Guide for the Perplexed

James Forsyth

© 2001 Novalis, Saint Paul University, Ottawa, Canada

Cover: Allegro 168inc.
Layout: Caroline Gagnon

Business Office:
Novalis
49 Front Street East, 2nd Floor
Toronto, Ontario, Canada
M5E 1B3

Phone: 1-800-387-7164 or (416) 363-3303
Fax: 1-800-204-4140 or (416) 363-9409
E-mail: novalis@interlog.com

National Library of Canada Cataloguing in
Publication Data

Forsyth, James, 1930-
  Catholicism revisited: a guide for the
perplexed

Includes bibliographical references.
ISBN 2-89507-169-1

  1. Theology, Doctrine–Popular works. I. Title.

BX1754.F67 2001      230      C2001-902306-5
Printed in Canada.

We acknowledge the financial support of the Government of Canada through the Book Publishing Industry Development Program (BPIDP) for our publishing activities.

*Life is a garden*
*in which some people look at the flowers*
*while others study the roots.*

To Betty,
who taught me to look at flowers.

*We should never belittle our own salvation, for if we do, we are saying that what we hope for is insignificant! Those who think it really is of no great value are wrong; but so are we if we are little aware of whence, by whom and whither we are called.*

(Anonymous second-century homily)

# CONTENTS

# INTRODUCTION

In his 1993 book, *The Moved and the Shaken,* author Ken Dryden uncovers the drama to be found in the most ordinary of lives by chronicling the day-to-day life of a very ordinary Canadian. Frank Bloye is a middle-aged man with a wife and three children. He lives in the suburbs and works as a customer service representative for a large oil company. His concerns and anxieties are equally "ordinary": marriage, home, children, family budget, job security. Religion – or at least faith – is also a factor in Frank's life. Some of his most treasured memories of his Catholic boyhood include serving as an altar boy; altar service is obviously something at which he excelled. His comments further reveal that the faith he acquired in childhood is still a great motivating factor in his life and something that brings him "inner peace." Frank's life is clearly rooted to a great extent in his relationship with God. Of his relationship to the Church, however, Dryden writes:

> He doesn't go to Church much now…. Only [his daughter] Stephanie shows interest sometimes and, when she does, he goes with her. Otherwise on Sunday mornings he just putters around his night darkened house and garden. But if it seems that his mother would roll over in her grave if she knew, maybe she wouldn't. He questions more than before, believes the Church is wrong about many things, abortion and birth control included. He may believe in his own free will to decide most things himself, still, with the Church as his

counsel, he is as imbued with religion now as
he was as an altar boy thirty years ago.[1]

Frank Bloye is what I would call a "perplexed Catholic."
Like Frank, there are many who have been raised as Catholics
and retain some of the faith-inspired values of the Roman
Catholic tradition and yet feel alienated from the Church. These
are people for whom the Church and its teachings have become
irrelevant or problematic. Perplexed Catholics are not confined
to those who have stopped going to church; they are also found
among those who attend Mass regularly. Some of the reasons for
these feelings of alienation or estrangement from the Church are
not difficult to find: some Catholics have ceased to find in the
Church's preaching, teaching and worship the kind of spiritual
enrichment they are seeking. Not finding the means of spiritual
growth in their own religious tradition, they look to other
traditions or give up on "organized religion" altogether and
explore secular systems of spirituality. How many times have
you heard someone say, "I'm not religious (i.e., I don't go to
church), but I try to live a spiritual life"? Others perceive the
doctrinal and moral teachings of the Church to be demanding
blind faith and unthinking obedience. Still others feel that, in
spite of the widespread use of the term "parish community,"
they experience none of that sense of belonging normally
associated with being part of a community.

At one point in the play *Auntie Mame* the flamboyant
Mame shares with us a bit of her philosophy of life. "Life," she
intones, "is a banquet and most poor sons of bitches are starving
to death." I believe that these words describe the plight of
perplexed Catholics. They are the inheritors of a religious tradition rich in spiritual and moral wisdom and yet they are starving.
A message of salvation intended to ground and enrich their lives
seems to have produced only guilt and confusion. Religion
seems to have become a burden despite the fact that the Saviour
promised a yoke that was easy and a burden that was light. The
premise of this book is that one of the roots of the feelings of
alienation that perplexed Catholics experience is a distorted

---

[1] *The Moved and the Shaken* (New York: Viking, 1993), p. 102.

understanding of the Catholic tradition, of the doctrinal and moral teachings of the Church and of the role of the Church in Catholic life. In many cases, the consequence of such misunderstandings is that Catholics end up with exaggerated notions of what is expected of them in the way of faith and obedience. In short, they are "more Catholic than the pope." More than 30 years after Vatican II, the meaning of faith and of its role in the process of salvation as well as the role of the Church's moral teachings in the lives of Catholics is still widely misunderstood.

The purpose of this book is to *make sense* of the words in which the Christian message has been transmitted to us in the Catholic tradition. There are no substitutes for words like sin, grace, faith, salvation and eternal life. The Christian message cannot be understood without an understanding of their meaning. A distorted understanding of these words is the result of not being able to relate them to anything in one's human experience. And yet each of them refers to a very definite kind of human experience. I believe that we can begin to discover their authentic meaning by examining the human experiences to which they refer. These words cease to have real meaning when their theological meaning is divorced from the human experiences to which they refer. Catholic tradition maintains that there is an analogy between the divine and the human; that one can learn something about God by examining human life and experience. If, therefore, God is revealed to us as our Father, surely we can apply to him the best qualities of a human father. If the grace of God means the *love* of God, we can understand something of the meaning of grace from what we know about human love. And if salvation means "healing," surely this tells us something about how salvation is experienced.

The principle of analogy implies that the language we use to speak of God and to transmit the Christian tradition has a real meaning. Even though the words we use to describe the reality of God and the mystery of salvation fall far short of exhausting the meaning of those realities, the human meaning of those words nevertheless says something real and true. Why then do we insist on giving those words some kind of esoteric meaning unrelated to our human experience? The principle of analogy implies that the words of the Christian vocabulary – since they have real meaning – are to be taken seriously. It is the purpose of this book to do just that: to understand God as father by exploring the meaning of human parenthood; to understand the grace or love of God by exploring the nature of human love; to understand the promise of eternal life by exploring the human experience of genuine life, and so on. By linking these words of an ancient tradition to a contemporary psychological understanding of the human experiences they represent, we shall perhaps be imitating the scribe who, in Jesus' words, "brings out from his storeroom things both new and old" (Matthew 13:52).

Those reading this book who are looking for an exhaustive treatment of Catholicism or an in-depth theological discussion of the topics we are dealing with will be disappointed. Those looking for a "bitch and moan" adolescent diatribe against Church authority will be equally disappointed. Ditto for those expecting an elaborate defence of Church teachings. The aim of this book is not to defend, convert or instill faith but simply to make some progress towards the understanding that faith constantly seeks. Its modest aim is to arrive at a distortion-free understanding of the Catholic Christian tradition by exploring and rethinking with the reader a few major themes in that tradition. If the Christian message is distorted and misunderstood, it will never have its intended liberating and enriching impact on human life. And if that message is misunderstood, it is important to revisit it and reaffirm its essential meaning.

The reflections that make up this book represent my understanding of what makes the Catholic Christian tradition spiritually and humanly enriching. It is my hope that, in these reflections, the "perplexed Catholic" will discover that, while being Catholic is a matter of choice, being perplexed doesn't help anyone. To this end, I invite the reader to put aside for the moment all preconceived ideas and to follow the example of the Virgin Mary who "pondered these things in her heart." It is, after all, no accident that she is hailed in our tradition as the "seat of wisdom," since wisdom is a matter of the heart as well as the intellect.

# Introduction

In the first century, St. Ignatius of Antioch warned his followers against false doctrine: "I pray you – not really I, but Christ's love through me – to eat only the food of Christ and to abstain from the alien food of heresy" (*Letter to the Trallians*). Notice Ignatius' emphasis: it is really the loving concern of Christ that urges us to understand our faith correctly. To live with a distorted understanding of the faith is like eating an "alien food" that fails to provide the spiritual nourishment one needs. No Christian should have to live such an undernourished life.

# PART I
# GOD AND RELIGION

The phenomenon of religion seems to persist even though its irrelevance has been frequently proclaimed. It has been judged at various times by philosophers as rationally untenable, by scientists as irrelevant, and by social scientists as a purely sociological or psychological phenomenon. Today the verdict on religion is not left to scholars and scientists. Lots of ordinary folks judge it to be irrelevant, inferior or even an obstacle to "spirituality." I suggest, therefore, that we begin our revisiting of Catholic Christianity by asking three questions about it:

1) As a "revealed" religion, is it necessary?

2) As a means of achieving spiritual goals, does it "work"?

3) How is the reality of the God who is the object of its faith to be understood?

# 1. IS RELIGION NECESSARY?

Helen is a middle-aged wife and mother. Her Catholic upbringing and schooling have left her with what seems to be an indelible Catholic identity. Her Catholicism seems to be "bred in the bone." She has tried to give her grown children a similar upbringing and schooling, but sees no recognizable Catholic identity in them. It seems that nothing could be less relevant to their lives than the teaching and worship of the Church. Truth to tell, she often shares their feelings of alienation from the Church. She grew up in the pre-Vatican II Church, but was generally enthusiastic about the changes introduced by the Council. In time, however, she began to experience a sense of loss and confusion. She still attends Mass, but it no longer seems to play the central role in her life that it once did. The revised liturgy does not seem to arouse the same range of emotions or convey the same sense of the sacred as the old Latin Mass. This despite the fact that her mind tells her that it makes perfectly good sense to celebrate Mass in the language of the people. Nevertheless, when she attends Mass now, she no longer has the feeling that she is going to a sacred place to participate in a sacred rite. The whole thing seems to have taken on the atmosphere of a "folksy" town hall meeting. The lector's reading is often garbled; the hymns are often trite; and last week she received communion from someone wearing a Chicago Bulls T-shirt. Although she finds the idea of "celebrating as a community" more appealing than "fulfilling one's Sunday obligation," she experiences little sense of community with her fellow parishioners and wonders how many Catholics (including herself) really understand what they are celebrating.

Helen also seems to have lost the sense of the Church as a moral compass in her life. She realizes that, in the end, it is the responsibility of her own conscience to make moral decisions. Nevertheless, she still looks to the Church as a source of moral guidance. Yet she seldom, if ever, hears explanations of the Church's moral teachings from the pulpit. Like others of her age, she feels she is losing her moral grounding. The old Catholic certainties seem to have given way to a call to more personal moral responsibility. Helen's problem, however, is that her moral life seems to have been one of obedience to the Church's moral teachings. No one ever taught her how to make responsible moral decisions while remaining a loyal Catholic; and no one is teaching her now.

Helen is pleased that the post-Vatican II Church has stopped treating the world – her world – as if it were nothing more than an enormous "occasion of sin." She fully accepts the emphasis on the life of faith not as a world-escaping "me and God" relationship, but as an active reaching out to the world and its needs. At the same time, she feels the need of spiritual nourishing and strengthening in order to live out such a faith commitment. That spiritual nourishment, however, no longer seems to come from her participation in the life and worship of the Church. Many traditional forms of Catholic piety (e.g., rosary, benediction, stations of the cross) have disappeared or been de-emphasized. Perhaps it is just as well; perhaps they were just part of an historical phase in the life of the Church. Nothing much, however, seems to have replaced them. Some of Helen's contemporaries have turned to alternate sources to satisfy their spiritual needs: feminine spirituality, charismatic groups, Buddhist meditation, self-help literature or "new age" spirituality. Helen, however, continues to seek spiritual strength from her faith and her Church. Therefore, she dutifully attends Mass every Sunday where she exchanges the "sign of peace" with a group of strangers. But something is missing and she is beginning to wonder whether the trappings of religion are necessary for her to be the person she wants to be and live the life she wants to live. Could she not simply pursue her own private relationship with God? Is religion – in the sense of "organized" religion – really necessary?

Helen's experience is not unique; it is repeated countless times in the lives of those I call perplexed Catholics. But why does Helen persist in her Catholic faith? Why does she continue to be what the media like to call a "devout" Catholic? Cynics might suggest that she is merely acting out of lifelong habit or that she is motivated by guilt. At a deeper level, however, there are at least two other factors at work. First, Helen genuinely believes the basic Christian proposition that God has revealed himself in the person of Jesus Christ. She wants to be a part of that community – the Church – which proclaims, celebrates and responds to that revelation. We shall return to this point later, but first I want to suggest a second factor at work in Helen's religious life. Helen still believes that her religion is the best way to satisfy the spiritual needs she experiences and to pursue the spiritual values she believes in. From a human, psychological point of view, people are religious not only because God has revealed himself, but also because, in responding to that revelation, they want to fulfill the spiritual dimension of their humanity. Through religion, they try to live a richer, more satisfying life. Helen's experience suggests that people adhere to or abandon organized religion on the basis of whether or not it fulfills their deeply felt spiritual needs.

But what are these deeply felt spiritual needs? Helen might reply to this question as follows: "I want to be close to God, to feel the assurance of his love and protection. I want to live a life that has meaning and purpose. I want to have a loving relationship with my husband and children. I want to be part of a caring community and help to create a better world. I want to know and understand myself and experience inner peace of mind and heart and be a better, more complete person." This answer contains an implicit acknowledgment that she experiences a certain feeling of separation or alienation from God, from her family and community and even from her own self. Why does she turn to religion to overcome this sense of separation? According to one derivation, the word "religion" comes from the Latin verb *religare*, which means "to bind again." The function of religion is to bind together what has been separated: to make whole again what has been shattered or fragmented. Does not Helen's answer reveal that this is exactly what she looks for in her religion? She wants the inner peace that comes from a sense of personal wholeness: a healing of the inner turmoil and dividedness that prevent her from being the person she wants to be. She wants to overcome interpersonal enmities, tensions and misunderstandings and experience true solidarity with her family and community. Finally, she wants to overcome everything that separates her from God and to feel at one with the One who is the source not only of her life, but of its ultimate meaning and purpose.

It is important to remember that there is nothing particularly "religious" about this desire to overcome separation and alienation. It is a *human* desire to overcome what is essentially a *human* problem. It is part and parcel of human existence. What does it mean to be human? What is the characteristic of human life that distinguishes it from all other forms of earthly life? Surely the answer is the quality of self-awareness. To use psychoanalyst Erich Fromm's phrase, human life is "life aware of itself." Self-awareness means that people are able to take control of and responsibility for their own lives. They are not simply driven by instinctual impulses or slaves to an instinctual pattern of existence. Consequently, the human experience of alienation and separation seems to be accompanied by a sense of personal responsibility. Why must the lack of personal integrity, or enmity towards another person, or lack of meaning and purpose in our lives be accompanied by a sense of guilt? If these things are part of human existence, why can't we simply pass them off as "only human"? While feelings of alienation are indeed human, the accompanying feelings of guilt are a manifestation of the deep conviction that this is not the way we were meant to live. The alienation felt in such circumstances is a matter of fate – it is inevitable – and yet it is also a source of guilt because one is aware of a degree of personal responsibility for that state of alienation.

This aspect of the human condition is what the Church calls "original sin." It is an inevitable part of human existence for which we nevertheless feel guilty. Helen's explanation of what she seeks in her religion reveals that she – like everyone else – experiences this human condition of alienation on three levels.

1. *Self-alienation*: Consider first the ways in which people become alienated from themselves. Self-awareness creates the possibility of achieving a sense of personal identity. Everyone wants to become that unique, autonomous individual he or she was meant to be. This, however, is easier said than done when we consider all those social forces that pressure us to conform to society's dominant beliefs, ideas, values, prejudices, attitudes, tastes, ways of acting, speaking, dressing, etc. In the eagerness to belong and be accepted we tend to conform. While a certain degree of conformity is necessary and healthy, there is a point at which the role we want to play and the image we want to project take the place of the person we really are. The result is a loss of contact with our true self. To borrow St. James' example, it is

"like looking at your own features in a mirror and then, after a quick look, going off and immediately forgetting what you looked like" (James 1:24). The conformist has been described as a person "who wants to be a somebody by being like everybody, which makes him a nobody." Erich Fromm underlines the personal responsibility we feel for this type of alienation when he says, "There is nothing of which we are more ashamed than of not being ourselves, and there is nothing that gives us greater pride and happiness than to think, to feel, and to say what is ours."[2]

Another source of self-alienation is the separation between my ideal self – the self I ought and want to be – and the self I actually am. If the Christian message of God's love for us is difficult to believe, perhaps this is because we find it difficult to love ourselves. The golfer throwing away his putter in disgust after missing an easy putt is a metaphor for life. We frequently berate and punish ourselves for our mistakes and failings far more than others punish us. The tension between self-love and self-contempt seems to be at the root of so much destructive behaviour. The sense of self-alienation is further reinforced by the awareness that my conscious self is not my total self. The very fact that we speak of the "unconscious" implies that there is a dimension of the self from which the conscious self is separated or estranged. This further means that I am often unaware of the true motives for my behaviour; that I am, to some extent, unaware of my undesirable faults and traits; that I am living with only a fragment of my total self. In short, I am not "whole." Self-alienation, therefore, is precisely this sense of separation from one's true, better and total self. Hence, all the great religions have proclaimed – in one form or another – the maxim "Know thyself." Whether it looks to religion or to another source of healing, the divided, fragmented, incomplete self looks to be made whole. When Helen looks to her religion as a source of self-knowledge and inner peace in order to become a better person, she is seeking to heal this sense of inner dividedness.

2. *Alienation from others*: Self-awareness and individuality are also the root cause of feelings that can alienate people from each other. Such feelings are an innate aspect of our human

---

2 *Escape from Freedom* (New York: Avon, 1965), p. 288.

existence. Loneliness, as anyone can attest, does not simply result from the absence of others. Indeed, the deepest feelings of loneliness are often experienced when we are surrounded by other people. Again, part of the experience of life is to be constantly reminded of how limited are our efforts to know and understand another. Even the most intimate relationships are fraught with misunderstandings. That same sense of separation seems to be at the root of those secret enmities that can cause people to take pleasure in the misfortunes of others; of the need to put down others in order to enhance our own status; or of ethnic and racial hatreds. The advances in communications technology seem merely to reinforce the basic problems we have in our attempts to communicate at this deeply human level.

Individual consciousness, then, not only separates people from that part of the self that remains unconscious; it can also separate us from each other. Conscious individuality means that I am aware of myself as a unique person with a sense of personal identity. In the manner of God's answer to Moses (Exodus 3:14), I can say, "I am who I am." But God can say this without experiencing that sense of alienation from others that accompanies self-awareness. In the Christian view, this is so because God is a trinity of persons. In other words, when God says "I" God means three persons. However, when I say, "I am who I am," I am in effect saying, "I am I and not you." To be a unique individual is to be, to some extent, unlike others and, therefore, separated or alienated from others. This feeling of alienation is the inevitable hindrance to even the best efforts to build community, to communicate, to love, to understand, to achieve intimacy. Fifty thousand people rising as one to give their favourite athlete a standing ovation may have a fleeting sense of the kind of cohesiveness and unity of purpose that create community. The fact that we refer to them as "fans" – a contraction of "fanatics" – might be an indication of how rare such an experience is. Helen looks to her religion for an experience of true community, for a healing of the alienation that separates her from others. That she will not find a perfect community there simply attests to the fact that the Church is not the fully realized kingdom of God.

23

3. *Alienation from God.* Individual self-awareness, then, is a two-sided coin. On the one hand, it is the source of a sense of individuality and uniqueness without which it is impossible to be truly human. On the other hand, it gives rise, of necessity, to feelings of isolation, and therefore separation, not only from others but also from the deepest dimensions of our own self. This same sense of isolation also carries with it feelings of powerlessness and inadequacy. The isolated individual experiences all the limitations that are part of being human, of being finite. Herein lies the root of a third level of separation. As finite beings we are separated from what is infinite; as relative to and conditioned by time and space we are separated from what is absolute and unconditioned. For the religious person, this translates into a sense of separation from God, since the religious person has given this name to what is infinite and absolute. For the non-religious person or the atheist, there is still a sense of separation from what God represents: life's ultimate meaning, purpose and destiny. For both religious and non-religious, this feeling of separation may be experienced as feelings of meaninglessness, doubt and cynicism. The human mind longs for ultimate and comprehensive knowledge, but human knowledge is limited and fragmented. It wants to know if there is any ultimate meaning to our existence, or indeed, if there is any meaning at all. And how will it all end? Is there life beyond death? Is there a meaning to one's life beyond paying off the mortgage or building up a healthy retirement fund? Whether people are religious or not, they want their lives to be part of a meaningful whole; to have meaning within some ultimate context. For the religious person, God is the ultimate source of meaning and purpose. Thus Helen, above and beyond all human resources, needs to be "close to God" to give meaning to her life.

Neither God nor religion are necessary for people to know that the human condition is one of separation or estrangement. The threefold sense of separation – from self, from others and from what is ultimate in being and meaning – is a fact of daily experience. It is a constant reminder that life is not everything it should be: that our human life, as we actually experience it, is limited and incomplete. If life were perfect – if it were everything it should be – everyone would be a fully integrated person, in full and loving communion with his or her fellow human beings and fully aware of life's ultimate meaning and its ultimate destiny. Alas, it isn't so, but when people describe even their modest successes in this direction as "getting it together," it is an acknowledgment that the fundamental problem of our existence is separation. It also reveals that the awareness of what life ought to be creates a desire for life as it ought to be – for the so-called "good life." When the shallower meanings of this phrase have been disposed of, it is discovered that at the heart of each person's religious or spiritual life is a desire to "reconnect," to heal the various forms of alienation that afflict and limit one's human existence. The fundamental human desire is for a life free of all these limitations, for life in all its potential fullness. Surely Jesus was responding to this desire when he proclaimed that he had come so that we might "have life and have it to the full" (John 10:10). This human desire is sometimes referred to as a desire for *transcendence*. It is the desire to "transcend" or go beyond or rise above the actual conditions of human existence. This desire is the human root of religion and spirituality. In fact, it could be argued that it constitutes the spiritual dimension of our human nature. The human spiritual quest, therefore, might be described as a desire to achieve a level of existence in which the limitations and incompleteness of our actual life are "transcended"; in which all forms of separation and estrangement are healed; in which life is experienced in all its fullness, not as limited and fragmented. In religious language this becomes the desire for "salvation."

Now the important thing to note about this fundamental human desire for transcendence is that it is not specifically religious. Although it coincides with the aims of religion, the desire itself is a human desire. As such, it may be expressed in a religious or a non-religious/secular way – in art, literature, music, etc. By way of illustration consider the following comparison. The famous gospel singer Mahalia Jackson used to sing a song called "Wake up in Glory," in which she expressed her Christian belief that when she dies she will wake up in heaven with Jesus and see the face of God. The song describes heaven as a place where all the limitations of earthly life are left behind: "All my troubles will be gone / And I'll be free from sin at last / And I'll leave all my sorrows here below." Here the desire for transcendence is expressed in the explicitly religious language of faith. The same desire, however, may be expressed in a non-religious way. In the film *The Wizard of Oz*, for example, Judy Garland sings the popular classic "Over the Rainbow" – a song that expresses that same desire for transcendence, but in the purely secular language of a child's fantasy: "Someday I'll wish upon a star / And wake up where the clouds / Are far behind me / Where troubles melt like lemon drops / Away above the chimney tops / That's where you'll find me." Here it is not heaven, but the mythical land of Oz that promises to take young Dorothy beyond the limitations of everyday life in Kansas. The film even portrays it in bright technicolour as distinct from the drab black and white of Kansas.

It is worth noting that in both these examples the desire for transcendence is localized; it becomes the desire for a *place* (heaven, Oz). Why is this so? It seems that the object of this desire – a new level of existence – is so unlike one's actual existence that it must be in a place other than our present world. This is particularly true of religious language that speaks of heaven, the promised land, the new Jerusalem, the kingdom of God, etc. Even in the realm of political and social reform we sometimes fall back on this kind of religious language. Who can forget Martin Luther King's use of the imagery of the promised land in the struggle for civil rights? What human beings seek, both religiously and humanly, is such a radical transformation of individuals and society that it can only be described in this kind of metaphorical language. It is nothing short of what the New Testament calls a "new creation." As already noted, this desire for transcendence is not intrinsically or exclusively religious. The most that can be said is that, since this desire is rooted in human nature, human beings can be described as "naturally religious." It is human to want to achieve whatever is meant by going to heaven, finding the promised land, creating a Utopia, or travelling down the yellow brick road.

This fundamental desire, which is intrinsic to human nature, seeks the fullness of life. It pursues this goal by trying to heal the threefold separation that is also intrinsic to human nature: separation from self, from others and from God as the ultimate source of life and its meaning. Since this desire is not specifically religious, it is probably best described as "spiritual." Whether religious or not, humans are spiritual beings with spiritual needs and aspirations. Hence the frequently heard statement "I am not religious (i.e., I don't go to church) but I try to live a spiritual life." Some of Helen's friends who have given up on "organized" religion and have opted for alternative, "secular" forms of spirituality might make such a statement. It is important, however, not to think of religion and spirituality as two separate pursuits. Today there seems to be a widespread assumption that spirituality is something other than religion, something that "transcends" religion. This is true only in the sense that religion may be considered as only one way of expressing spirituality and satisfying spiritual needs. It is, however, a valid way of doing so. Attempts have been made, for instance, to describe Mother Teresa as a dedicated social worker whose humanitarianism somehow transcended and had little to do with her religion. While this tended to make her the darling of "liberal chic" circles, it was a description emphatically rejected by the "saint of the gutters." It is very clear that Mother Teresa's spirituality is deeply rooted in her frankly orthodox Catholic faith.

Now if the spiritual quest is an attempt to overcome the various forms of alienation that beset human existence, then it may be described more positively as the pursuit of three basic values: (1) *Wholeness or Integrity*. This refers to the desire to be reunited with one's true, better and more complete self. It is the desire to overcome inner conflict and to experience inner peace and harmony. (2) *Community*. This is the desire to go beyond one's isolated sense of self; to overcome the inevitable sense of alienation from others that accompanies self-awareness. It is the deeply felt need to forge bonds of community with others. (3) *Ultimacy*. I use this word to denote the search for ultimate reality, truth and meaning and a sense of ultimate destiny: "No man is an island." Life is lived within a network of work, family, society, etc., thus creating a context that gives life meaning. The religious or spiritual quest is the search for an ultimate context that gives life an ultimate meaning. Psychologists have recognized this need. Gordon Allport (1897–1967) described God and religion as putting one's life in a "supreme context," thereby contributing to the attempt to "enlarge and complete" one's personality.[3] Viktor Frankl (1905–1997), who considered

---

[3] *The Individual and His Religion* (New York: Macmillan, 1950), p. 161.

"responsibleness" the hallmark of being human, found a similar psychological meaning in religious belief. For the religious person, God is the one to whom we are ultimately responsible.[4]

What has been said of the desire to overcome human alienation or estrangement can be said of the pursuit of these three basic values. They can be pursued in either religious or secular ways; they are both religious and human values. This suggests a twofold conclusion concerning religion: (1) From this purely human and psychological point of view (i.e., in the light of our human spiritual needs), religion is not strictly "necessary" since its goals may be pursued in a secular/humanistic way. (2) Nevertheless, it should also be clear that religion – at its best – is not something contrary to or "tacked on" to our human nature. Its call to greater wholeness, community and ultimacy corresponds to the deepest aspirations of the human heart. If these aspirations remain unfulfilled, the human heart suffers the anxiety of alienation and meaninglessness. It was the experience of this kind of anxiety that led St. Augustine to say to God, "You have made us for yourself and our heart is restless until it rests in you."[5]

What, then, is the answer to the question "Is religion necessary?" I have already suggested that, from the point of view of expressing our spirituality, fulfilling our spiritual needs or pursuing spiritual values (all of which may be done in a non-religious, secular way), it must be maintained that religion is not necessary. Religious believers do not have a monopoly on spirituality or on the spiritual values of wholeness, community and ultimacy. For religious believers, however, the answer is not so simple. Their religion is not merely one of many freely chosen options for satisfying a personal, spiritual need. It does not proceed from an inner need only; it is also the result of a challenge or call from beyond the self. Christians, Jews and Muslims all believe that, while their faith is a freely made human act, it is also a response to God's revelation of himself and to his intervention in the life of humanity. Helen, for instance, believes that God is revealed in the person of Jesus Christ and feels a need to respond to that revelation. Thus there is a sense in which her religion is "necessary" for her. The true believer is not

---

[4] *The Unconscious God* (New York: Simon and Schuster, 1975), chap. 5.

[5] *Confessions,* Book 1, chap. 1.

religious primarily to fulfill human needs – spiritual or otherwise. If this were so, religion would lose its compelling and challenging character. Religion may indeed be the source of inner peace of mind, human fellowship, meaning and purpose. One is not religious, however, only because of these benefits. In fact, the commitment of faith may be made contrary to all considerations of human wisdom or human advantage. Religion confronts us, challenges us and calls us into a faith relationship with a transcendent God. The believer responds with faith and commitment.

The fulfillment of those human spiritual needs that we associate with religion must be seen as a consequence or side effect of this religious commitment. Even Jesus attributed the physical cures he performed to the faith of the petitioners ("Your faith has saved you"). This is not just a religious truth; it is a human, psychological truth as well. Happiness, for example, which everyone desires, nevertheless cannot be directly pursued – the United States constitution notwithstanding – but is experienced only as a consequence or side effect of successfully responding to life's challenges. Faith is not calculating. It does not ask, "What's in it for me?" It has to be self-forgetful in order to be humanly and spiritually fulfilling. As Jesus put it, "Anyone who loses his life for my sake will find it" (Matthew 10:39). For the religious believer, then, religion has the character of necessity since it is a response to a call that is found to be compelling and challenging. It must be remembered, however, that this is a subjective judgment on the part of the believer: "My religion is necessary *for me*." It cannot be turned into an objective judgment: "My religion is necessary *for everyone*." Those fundamentalist Christians who want to make explicit faith in Christ and Christian baptism prerequisites for salvation would do well to ponder the words of Christ himself in Luke 9:49-50. The apostle John wanted to stop a man who was casting out devils in the name of Jesus. His reason? "He is not with us." In other words, he is not a member of our group, of our "church." Jesus' reply is emphatic: "You must not stop him; anyone who is not against you is for you." Those who seek spiritual values in a non-religious way are not, for that reason, "against" religion, since the goals they pursue are the goals of religion itself.

## 2. DOES CHRISTIANITY WORK?

In Chapter 1 the question about religion was answered as follows: The goals or values of religion (wholeness, community, ultimacy) are also human goals and values and, consequently, may be pursued and expressed in a secular, non-religious way. From this perspective, religion is not necessary. This conclusion was qualified by noting that the faith commitment of the religious believer is experienced as necessary or compelling in that it is a response to a call and a challenge from a transcendent God who takes the initiative and intervenes in the life of humanity. It was also noted that, for the religious believer, the satisfaction of these human, spiritual needs is not directly sought but is experienced as a consequence or side effect of the religious commitment.

While all this may be true in theory, the perplexed Catholic, I believe, asks a more pragmatic question: In the case of the Christian faith commitment, does this consequence or side-effect take place? Does Christianity (including Catholic Christianity) fulfill the spiritual needs of those who make this faith commitment? Does it help them to achieve a new level of existence? Does it help them to overcome the various forms of separation from the desired fullness of life? Does the Christian experience transform people in such a way that they experience greater personal wholeness, a greater sense of community with others and a greater sense of oneness with God as the source of life, meaning and purpose? In other words, apart from the question of whether Christianity is true, does it work? Is it "true" in this subjective, pragmatic sense? Of course, each Christian will have to answer this question for himself or herself. The only question that can be dealt with in a general way is the question of what the Christian message and the believer's response to it are *intended* to accomplish. This requires an understanding of what the Christian message is. To this end, I suggest that some reflection on two pertinent parables of Jesus would be helpful.

1. *The Labourers in the Vineyard* (Matthew 20:1-16). This parable is familiar to all Christians, but for those with a legalistic mindset it is a tough nut to crack. A landowner needed

labourers to work in his vineyard. At daybreak he went to the marketplace and hired a group of casual labourers and agreed to pay them a set wage. At various other times of the day (the third, sixth, ninth and eleventh hours) he went out again, hiring more labourers each time and promising them "a fair wage." At the end of the day all the labourers – regardless of the length of their shift – received the same wage as the first group to be hired. Even those who had been hired at the eleventh hour and had worked only one hour received a full day's wages. Those who had worked the whole day resented this and complained. The landowner reminds them that they had not been treated unjustly; they received the wages to which they had agreed. He then added: "Take your earnings and go. I choose to pay the last-comer as much as I pay you. Have I no right to do what I like with my own? Why be envious because I am generous?" And Jesus comments: "Thus will the last be first and the first last."

2. *The Prodigal Son* (Luke 15:11-32). In this even more familiar parable, the younger of two sons asked his wealthy father to give him, in advance, his share of the father's estate. When the father agreed, the son "got together everything he had and left for a distant country where he squandered his money on a life of debauchery." When he had spent all his money and the country in which he was living began to experience hard times, the prodigal son hit rock bottom. He managed to find work feeding the pigs of a local farmer. Realizing that the pigs were better fed than he was, he "came to his senses" and returned to his father, not to be reinstated as his son, but to work as one of his hired hands. But the father would have none of this. He was overjoyed at his son's return: "This son of mine was dead and has come back to life; he was lost and was found." The scruffy, dishevelled son is dressed in the finest clothes, the fatted calf is killed and a party is held to celebrate the son's return. The older son, however, refuses to join the celebration. He stands outside and sulks. He, the obedient, hard-working son for so many years, has never been recognized or rewarded in this way. Doesn't he deserve more than this wasteful, self-indulgent younger brother? The father can only answer: "My son, you are with me always and all I have is yours. But it was only right that we should celebrate and rejoice, because your brother here was dead and has come to life; he was lost and is found."

Most of us would have to admit that, on first hearing these parables, we tended to sympathize with the workers who had worked the whole day and with the prodigal son's older brother. Surely the workers who had put in more hours deserved a higher wage; and surely the older brother who had served his father so loyally deserved more than the prodigal son who had broken his father's heart. In both cases our sympathies were with those whom we felt to be *more deserving* according to a human standard of justice. If the parables are intended to illustrate the manner in which God deals with us, are we to draw the conclusion that God is capricious and unjust? When such a standard is applied we miss the point of the parables: God does not treat people according to human standards of strict justice. Consequently, when such standards are applied to an interpretation of these parables, what they say about our relationship with God is distorted. In this regard, two aspects of the parables are worth noting.

First, it is important to notice that in both parables those who appear to be undeserving never claim to deserve the reward they receive. Notice that the first group of vineyard workers hired entered into a contract to work a full day for a fixed wage. Those who were hired later in the day did not have the security of such a binding contract. They simply put their trust in the landowner's promise to pay them a "fair wage." They had no expectation of receiving a full day's wages. In the same way, the prodigal son did not expect, much less demand, to be welcomed back lovingly and joyfully as a returning son. He feels distinctly unworthy of such a reception and hopes only to find work as one of his father's servants. The hard-working older brother – like the hard-working vineyard workers – is resentful. In both cases the focus is on what they *deserve* as compared with those who are less deserving. If these parables speak about our relationship with God, it is, in the first instance, to contrast these two ways in which one may relate to God. Some relate to God in a legalistic way, believing that God will reward them with what they deserve by reason of their loyal service and virtuous life. Others – like the late-comers to the vineyard and the prodigal son – relate to God with a trusting faith, believing that God will reward them not on the basis of what they deserve but out of his loving mercy. Indeed, if God rewards us strictly according to what we deserve, most of us would have the distinct feeling of being in over our heads.

Second, both parables illustrate the fundamental nature of the Christian message, which is a message of *grace*. God does not deal with people according to strict justice. His love is not something to be earned and therefore deserved; it is given freely, gratuitously, unconditionally. If we think of our relationship with God as a legalistic one in which we have to earn God's favour and God's rewards are in proportion to what we think we deserve based on our human efforts, the result is a profound misunderstanding of the God who is revealed in Christ and a stunting of our human and spiritual growth. The vineyard workers who worked the whole day could not understand the landowner's generosity to the late-comers. Moreover, their legalistic attitude of strict justice filled them with resentment towards their fellow workers. They were unable to feel any happiness for these unemployed workers who finally got a break; they saw them as "welfare bums" who didn't deserve the "handout" they received. In the same way, the older brother cannot understand the father's forgiving generosity towards the prodigal son. He, too, is resentful. He isolates himself from the merrymaking – a prisoner of his own self-righteousness – and is unable to feel any happiness for his younger brother, who is finally beginning to get his life together.

In addition, therefore, to telling us something about God, these parables tell us something about ourselves. The more we think of our religion as a means of earning or deserving God's favour, the more we become preoccupied with our own merits or deservedness. To be thus preoccupied with earning something for myself means that I am preoccupied with myself. Such self-absorption is obviously an obstacle to the kind of selfless love of others that is the Christian moral ideal. Indeed, it tends to reinforce the sense of separation and isolation that characterizes the human condition and cuts us off from the experience of life's fullness. Christianity calls this human condition of separation or alienation "sin" or the state of "original sin." It is original in the sense of originating with human existence. It "goes with the territory"; it is part of being human, a fundamental aspect of the human condition. It is not the result of an accidental, catastrophic event at the beginning of human history, of Adam and Eve's unfortunate slip-up. The story of Adam and Eve and the "Fall" (Genesis 3) is a mythical expression of the reality of sin. To describe the state of sin as inherited from humanity's "first parents" is a mythical way of accounting for the universality of this condition. The myth, therefore, contains not an historical truth but a profound truth about the human condition. As Thomas Bokenkotter puts it: "Genesis' account of the Fall was obviously not intended as history but, rather, as a way of expressing the biblical author's awareness of a basic flaw in human nature."[6]

This flaw in human nature is what has been called the human condition of separation and alienation (from self, others and God). This is the fundamental meaning of sin in the sense of original sin. Both religion and spirituality aim at overcoming this state of separation and thus use the language of reunion or connectedness or oneness, of being reconnected with that from which we are separated. This is particularly true of the language describing mystical or ecstatic experiences. This notion of reunion or oneness belongs to the root meaning of the word "religion." The Christian message, then, is a message offering the possibility of reunion in this sense, since it is a message of *grace*. This message can be summed up in two words: sin and grace. What difference does it make that Jesus Christ was born, lived, died and rose from the dead? What effect does all this have on my life? St. Paul answers with this simple statement: "Where sin abounded, grace did much more abound" (Romans 5:20). Christ makes a difference for the Christian believer because in him is revealed the grace of God and grace is the remedy for sin, the healing of the human condition of separation. The Christian message, then, is a message of grace for those who live in a state of sin (separation).

To understand this statement in any way that is relevant to our human experience, it may be necessary to be open to a deeper understanding of the words "sin" and "grace." This may involve putting aside notions inherited from our childhood catechism and never revised. In the first place, the word "sin," in

---

[6] *Dynamic Catholicism: A Historical Catechism* (New York: Doubleday, 1992), p. 300.

this context, is not simply the singular of the word "sins": that is, offences against the moral law. It is the Christian word for the human condition of separation. It is a state, not an act or omission; the state from which we need to be redeemed by grace. Catholics of a certain age may protest that they have heard enough about sin to last a lifetime. Sin was something they were always confessing and for which they were forever making "reparation." The residue of all this is the well-known condition called "Catholic guilt." Unfortunately, the compensating message of God's forgiving love (grace) often got lost in the shuffle. At the same time, if sin is a fundamental aspect of the human condition (alienation), it is a reality that cannot be ignored. Without it, the Christian message of grace becomes meaningless. Like sin, grace is a state. It is a state that represents the overcoming or transcending of the state of sin. It represents, therefore, the goal of the spiritual quest – a new level of existence in which the limitations of one's ordinary existence (sin, separation) are overcome.

At this point one is almost tempted to apologize for the use of a term such as "original sin." There are those who, inspired by something they mistakenly identify as the "spirit of Vatican II," find this doctrine distasteful and guilt-inducing. They want to replace this emphasis on humanity's fallen, sinful condition and need for redemption with an emphasis on the goodness of human nature – seemingly unaware that the doctrine implies no denial of the essential goodness of human nature as created by God. So let us be clear on this point. The doctrine of original sin simply makes a statement about the human condition: namely, that in our actual human existence, we are separated or estranged from the essential goodness of our human nature; that we stand in need of the grace (love) of God to heal that separation and actualize our essential goodness. It seems to me that this fact needs no more graphic proof than the daily reports in the media of killings, genocide, terrorism, violence, spousal and child abuse, road rage, etc.

The Protestant theologian Paul Tillich[7] has suggested that, to understand how humans experience sin and grace, we

---

[7] *The Shaking of the Foundations* (New York: Scribners, 1948), chap. 19.

should understand sin as a state of separation, and grace as a state of reunion or reconciliation of what has been separated. The effect of grace, then, is to reunite or to make whole what is separated. Grace is intended to heal the threefold separation of the self from oneself, from others and from God. The Christian message is a message of salvation (healing of separation) because it is a message of grace. It is not unusual for Christians to speak of the healing or transforming power of grace; the premise of the Christian message is that this healing or transformation is achieved through grace rather than our human efforts. Of this transformation St. Bonaventure wrote in the 13th century: "How can such a transformation take place? By grace, not doctrine; by desire, not understanding; by prayerful pleading, not studious reading; through the Spouse, not teachers; through God, not man."[8]

How does grace bring about this healing or transformation? This question will be dealt with in more detail in a later chapter. For the moment, however, it is helpful to remember that the healing, transforming power of grace is simply the healing, transforming power of love. If we think of grace in this way, it may help to dispel those magical notions of grace as *something* God gives the believer and that effects changes in some mysterious, incomprehensible way. Let us begin with St. Paul's brief summation of the Christian message that is read at the Christmas midnight Mass: "God's grace has been revealed, and it has made salvation possible for the whole human race" (Titus 2:11). With the coming of Christ, God's grace is revealed. This statement becomes more intelligible if we remember that God's grace simply means God's love. But the force of the word "grace" is that God's love is gracious or gratuitous. It is a love given freely and unconditionally, not as a reward for anything good we have done or any virtue we possess. As St. Paul puts it: "What proves that God loves us is that Christ died for us while we were still sinners" (Romans 5:8). In other words, God's declaration of his love for us (the death of his son) was made before we had done anything to earn or deserve it. Like the late-comers to the vineyard and the prodigal son, we are undeserving recipients of God's love.

---

[8] *The Journey of the Mind to God,* chap. 7, no.6

What are the practical consequences of this? It means that – unlike the complaining vineyard workers and the prodigal son's older brother – we do not regard God's love as a reward to be earned by loyal and strenuous effort. It means that the whole Christian life and worship is not a strenuous effort to earn God's love through moral and religious observance; it is a grateful acknowledgment and joyful celebration of that love that has already been given freely, with no strings attached. The love of God is a *fait accompli* and it is fair to say that the whole Christian life is a reaction to that fact. People who dismiss Christianity on the grounds that it is just a lot of doctrine, ritual and moral rules seem to miss the point. The fundamental Christian message is that God loves everyone unconditionally; God's love does not have to be earned. Doctrine is a way of transmitting this basic message; ritual is a communal celebration of it; moral teachings are guidelines to help us live a life that is an appropriate response to God's revealed love. The problem arises when doctrine, ritual and moral teachings obscure rather than illuminate this message. Doctrine, ritual and moral teachings may evolve and develop over time; the basic Christian message of grace – of God's unconditional love – remains the same. "For reasons that escape us completely," writes Andrew Greeley, "the animating power of the universe claims to have fallen in love with us."[9]

Perhaps the closest human analogy to the love of God is the love of parents for a newborn child. Why do the parents lavish such love and affection on the newborn who, strictly speaking, has done nothing to earn such love? Because it is "natural"? Because the infant is appealingly small and helpless? Because he or she embodies the parents' love for each other? Whatever answer is given affirms the truth that love, unlike respect, admiration, etc., cannot be earned or deserved. Yet, in spite of this fact of daily human experience, the love and acceptance of God are often treated as something to be earned through strenuous moral and religious effort. If human beings can love one another unconditionally and receive each other's love with faith and trust, why should not God's love and the human response to it follow the same pattern? If God is our

---

[9] *The Great Mysteries* (New York: Seabury, 1976), p. 73.

father, surely he can love his children in the way human parents love their children. Jesus himself posed this question: "If you then, who are evil, know how to give your children what is good, how much more will the heavenly Father give the Holy Spirit to those who ask him" (Luke 11:13). The gift of the Holy Spirit is the gift of God's love. As St. Paul reminds us, "The love of God has been poured into our hearts by the Holy Spirit which has been given us" (Romans 5:5). If love is not something that can be earned, why do we make an exception of the love of God? On this point, Andrew Greeley writes, "We can no more merit [God's] forgiving love than we can merit existence. It is there ready for us to accept it. You cannot earn what is there for the asking."[10]

On the basis of the words of St. Paul, the Christian message might be summarized as the revelation of God's gratuitous, unconditional love (i.e., grace). "The grace of God has been revealed," St. Paul tells us. One Christmas Eve several years ago I tuned in to the telecast of Pope John Paul's midnight Mass. I noticed that, in his homily, he repeated several times the words *apparuit gratia* (grace has appeared). The pope was clearly emphasizing the fact that the revelation of God's grace – God's love in Christ – was the central meaning of and the reason for the Christmas celebration. We know of God's love because it has been revealed, not in words only but in the person of Christ. The appropriate response to this revelation is faith: a trusting belief in that love. Finally, this grace or love is so great (it "abounds") that it saves humanity from the effects of sin, the state of separation or alienation that is experienced as separation from self, from others, and from God or ultimate reality and meaning.

The saving effect of grace or the love of God is therefore the healing of this threefold separation. First, grace is the experience of reunion or reconciliation with God. To respond to God's unconditional declaration of love with faith means – as it does with human love – to be taken into a personal relationship with God (as his child). This relationship gives meaning and purpose to life and puts our lives into an ultimate context. Second, God's unconditional love and acceptance allow us to

---

[10] The Great Mysteries, p. 69.

acknowledge and accept ourselves completely, even the dark and rejected side of the self. Self-acceptance and, therefore, reunion with the rejected part of oneself follows from the experience of acceptance by another. If God loves and accepts me, I can love and accept myself. It goes without saying that this is also true on the purely human level. Self-acceptance and self-esteem are important ingredients of an emotionally healthy life. We do not, however, fashion them entirely on our own; we are dependent on the love and acceptance of others (parents, family, etc.) in order to achieve self-acceptance. Without the human experience of love and acceptance, my capacity for faith – for a trusting belief in God's love for me – may be impaired. Third, the experience of grace is an experience of reunion and reconciliation with others. The believer recognizes that all of humanity is the object of this same divine love and acceptance. Grace "has made salvation possible," writes St. Paul, "for the whole human race." I am called, therefore, to live a life that reflects not only the fact that God loves me but also the fact that God loves everyone else as well.

Does Christianity work? Does it heal the human condition of separation? It is clear that, in this life, the healing is partial and incomplete and in proportion to the depth of our faith. The intent of the Christian message is to heal the sinful human condition of separation, alienation and estrangement. And to the extent that it does this, salvation is taking place.

# 3. IS GOD REAL?

Many years ago, there was a Canadian television show called *The Great Debate*. Each week two scholars, politicians, social leaders or representatives of professions were invited to debate a particular question. At the end of the debate, the studio audience was invited to ask questions. On one of these occasions, Malcolm Muggeridge, the English critic and apologist, was invited to debate "the question of God" with Charles Templeton, an ex-minister of the United Church of Canada. During the question period, one indignant teenager pointed out that, during the whole course of the debate, neither man had bothered to *prove the existence of God*. In this young man's view, this oversight had in some way invalidated the whole debate and rendered it useless. The reaction of both debaters indicated how aware they were of the difficulty in explaining to such a young person why this was not the important question. Given the rapid intellectual development of adolescence, it is not surprising that this young man should over-intellectualize the question of God. Many adults have never outgrown this tendency. They act as if the "proofs" for the existence of God were the foundation of religion. If God can be proven to exist, then religion makes sense. If not, religion makes no sense. And yet, for truly religious people, this does not seem to be *the* question. The existence or non-existence of God is not a religious question; it is a philosophical question.

The reason for this is that faith is not the conclusion of a rational argument. One may fully accept the logic of an argument for the existence of God and yet not have faith. Faith, after all, is something deeper than intellectual belief. (See Chapter 4.) Almost one hundred years ago, the American philosopher/psychologist William James argued that both religious belief and unbelief are rooted not in the rational part of our nature but in our feelings, intuition and human experience. These are primary. Rational arguments in favour of belief or unbelief are secondary supports for convictions we already hold on emotional, intuitive, experiential grounds. "The unreasoned and immediate assurance," he wrote, "is the deep thing in us, the reasoned argument is but a surface exhibition. Instinct leads, intelligence does but follow."[11] Once belief is rooted in feeling and intuition and confirmed by one's life experience, James argued, rational arguments to the contrary are powerless to dispel it. Arguments *for* the existence of God are equally powerless to convert the non-believer. This is not to suggest that arguments for the existence of God serve no useful purpose. They are supporting evidence, but not the foundation or source of belief. If a person believes in God, it is because that person intuitively apprehends the reality of God and because this intuition is confirmed by his or her life experience. Rational arguments play a secondary role; they support a belief that is already there.

If the question of God and religion has been so "intellectualized" this is perhaps because faith has often been understood in an overly rational and intellectual way. Faith is the word we use to describe the response of one's whole person to God. (See Chapter 4.) It involves not just intellectual belief, but radical trust and moral commitment as well. Understood in this way, faith involves a real *conversion*; it has an impact on a person's life. Yet somehow faith is often understood as mere belief – the assent of one's mind to doctrine. Our life experience suggests, however, that what is merely intellectual – what is only in the mind – may have little if any impact on our everyday lives. How many Christians, for instance, can explain how belief in the doctrine of the Trinity has changed their lives? How did this intellectualizing of faith come about? I believe that, in part, it is due to the fact that at a certain point in time Christians began to ask a different kind of question about God and talk in a different way about God. For the early Christians, God was creator and Father; Jesus was their Lord, saviour and redeemer. Now all these terms – creator, Father, saviour, etc. – are descriptions of what God and Christ are *to us*; they describe the *function* of God and Christ in our lives. They answer an "existential" question: What do God and Christ mean for my human existence? During the fourth and fifth centuries, however, the Church was troubled by a series of *doctrinal* controversies. These centred mostly on

---

[11] *The Varieties of Religious Experience* (New York: Macmillan, 1961, c. 1902), p. 75.

the nature of Christ; ecumenical councils were required to define what the Church believed on these questions.

Each of the great ecumenical councils of the fourth and fifth centuries was convened to settle a particular theological dispute. The council of Nicea (in 325) affirmed the divinity of Christ in response to the teaching of Arius, who had argued that Christ was not divine but a "perfect creature." The council described Christ as "consubstantial" with the Father or, as we say when we recite the Nicene Creed, "one in being" with the Father. The council of Ephesus (in 431) upheld the validity of Mary's title of "Mother of God" by rejecting the teaching of Nestorius, who claimed that Mary was merely the mother of a human person (Jesus) in whom God dwelled. The council of Chalcedon (in 451) gave us the traditional formula for describing the nature of Christ – that he is one person with two natures: a human nature and a divine nature.

In these ecumenical councils and in the doctrinal controversies that occasioned them, the question about Christ is not simply the existential question (What is Christ for me?) but the more "ontological" question (What is Christ *in himself*? What is his inner nature? How could he be fully human and divine?). Why this preoccupation with such questions as the inner nature of Christ and his relationship with God the Father? Is it not sufficient for the Christian to simply know Christ as Son of God, as saviour and redeemer – that is, in terms of his function in the believer's life? Not only would this be sufficient, it is also the most important thing for the Christian to know. And yet there is something about the human mind that causes it to move from the functional question of what things are to us to the deeper question of what things are in themselves.[12] My knowledge of the computer I am using at this moment is limited to a knowledge of its function in my life and work. It would be perfectly natural for me to go beyond this functional question and ask the question of the computer's inner workings – how it does what it does – though I expect that to my technologically

---

[12] See John Courtney Murray S.J., *The Problem of God* (New Haven: Yale University Press, 1964) for a discussion of this as it relates to the question of God.

42

challenged mind this will remain as great a mystery as the mystery of God.

Though these ontological questions about the inner nature of God and of Christ are important, they are less relevant to the everyday life of the Christian than the more immediate question of what God and Christ mean to our human existence. Nevertheless, the Church had to deal with such questions since it is part of the Church's teaching function to define its belief and reject what it sees as distortions of that belief. Sometimes the Church has carried out this teaching function wisely, sometimes not so wisely. In spite of the frustration we might feel over doctrinal hairsplitting, I believe we can be grateful that the Church rejected the teachings of the second-century Gnostics, the fifth-century Manichaeans and the 12th-century Cathars, all of whom, in one way or another, held that the material world, the human body and sexuality were all inherently evil. On the other hand, considering the ridicule to which it has been subjected and all the distinctions and qualifications necessary to explain it, was it really worthwhile for the Church to define the doctrine of papal infallibility in 1870?

What these doctrinal controversies introduced into the Christian community was a preoccupation with "orthodoxy," or correct belief. If you accepted the official teachings of the Church on doctrinal matters, you were "orthodox"; if not, you were a "heretic." After the 11th-century schism that separated the Eastern and Western branches of Christendom, the Christians of the East became the "Orthodox Church" to differentiate themselves from their separated (i.e., heretical) brethren of the Western Church. While this concern for doctrinal clarity was important and necessary, it had an unfortunate side effect. It created an atmosphere in which it was easy to equate faith with orthodoxy. But there is more to faith than orthodox belief. (See Chapter 4.) This tendency to reduce the meaning of faith to *belief* – the assent of the mind to doctrinal propositions – is what I mean by the "intellectualizing" of faith, and it is still alive and well today.

Surely there is a direct link between this preoccupation with orthodox belief and St. Thomas Aquinas' 13th-century definition of faith as "the assent of the mind to divine truth...."

This is an understanding of faith that seems to have held sway in Catholic thought for the next seven centuries. Even today, when Catholics speak of having difficulty maintaining their faith, more often than not they are referring to a difficulty in giving this "assent of the mind." In other words, the difficulty is with some Church doctrine or moral teaching. On the other hand, if faith means not just intellectual belief but a total response to God's love as revealed in the person of Christ, not just assent of the mind but trusting belief in that divine love and acceptance, then would not the doubts that bedevil our faith be of a different kind? Would they not take the form of finding it hard to believe that the God of the universe wants to make me his child and love me as a father does; that he accepts me when I don't accept myself; that he forgives me when I can't forgive myself; that he shared my human condition and died a miserable death as visible proof of his love?

Here, then, are two ways of understanding faith. One way understands faith as a *trusting* response to God's declaration of love. The other understands faith as a *believing* assent of the mind to truths *about* God. Understood in the former sense, faith has the capacity to become the foundation of the whole Christian life because it has a liberating and transforming effect, just as believing in someone else's freely given love always has. Moreover, it has an impact on the believer's moral life and elicits a moral response. It affects the way one lives since one responds to love by loving in return. (See Chapter 6.) Understood in the latter sense (as mere belief), faith tends to be an intellectual activity divorced from everyday life. Intellectual belief does not have the transforming effect that faith should have, nor does it necessarily have an impact on the way one lives. It is possible to live a life completely at odds with one's intellectual beliefs. A further consequence is that, when the object of faith is a *truth* rather than a *person,* it sets up a conflict with rational/scientific truth.

Thomas Aquinas seems to have implicitly recognized the inherent inadequacy of this understanding of faith ("assent of the mind") in two ways. First, he distinguished between "unformed faith" (mere belief) and "faith formed by charity." Charity or love was seen as the "form" of faith "in so far as the act of faith is perfected and formed by charity." It was only "when accompanied by charity" that faith becomes "meritorious." In other words, something (charity or love) had to be added to faith (belief) to "perfect" it and make one a complete Christian. Second, faith understood as the assent of the mind to truths about God was seen as something that could be supported by arguments from reason. If faith had to do with beliefs about the existence and nature of God, then the next logical step was for theologians to speculate on whether anything about God could be known apart altogether from revelation (using only our unaided powers of human reason).

The result was an enterprise known as "natural theology," which attempted to know something of the existence and nature of God apart from God's own revelation of himself. This enterprise produced various rational arguments for the existence of God, the most influential of which are perhaps the famous "five ways" of Aquinas.[13] It is important to remember that Aquinas was writing for the Christian community, which already believed in God's existence on the basis of God's self-revelation. In advancing these five arguments, he was not advocating reason as an alternate way of knowing of God's existence. Aquinas did not believe that these arguments would convert a non-believer. They were meant to be a rational support for faith that already existed and to demonstrate that there was no inherent contradiction between faith and reason. It is primarily this attempt to synthesize faith and reason that accounts for Aquinas' greatness in the history of Christian thought.

So it happened that the Christian community came into the modern era with the conviction that its faith rested on a twofold foundation – revelation supported by arguments from reason. The philosophers and scientists of the 18th and 19th centuries, without necessarily denying the existence of God, rejected the idea that God's existence could be demonstrated by rational arguments. Our knowledge, they argued, is restricted; we can only know with certainty what belongs to the "phenomenal" or observable world (of which God is not a part), or only what can be known through the scientific method, through observable

---

[13] *Summa Theologiae*, Part 1, Question 2, Article 3.

and measurable data. How did the Christian world respond to this challenge? Orthodox Protestant theologians tended to agree, not for philosophical or scientific reasons but for theological reasons: God could not be truly known through reason because reason was subject to sin and consequently could only discover a God made in its own image. Their emphasis was on our absolute need for and dependence on God's revelation. Catholic theologians, while stressing that our faith is ultimately rooted in God's revelation, nevertheless continued to defend the validity of reason as a rational support for faith. In this way they were being faithful to the position of Thomas Aquinas, whose aim was to reconcile and synthesize faith and reason.

The premise of such an attempt at synthesis is that truth is one. Therefore, there cannot be a fundamental contradiction between the truths of faith and the truths of reason or, as we might say today, between religion and science. We err when we distort this principle to the point where there is only one kind of truth or one source of truth. There was a time when those who believed that religious truth was the only truth condemned scientists, such as Galileo, as heretics. Even today "creationists" try to turn the opening chapters of the Bible into a scientific account of the origin of the universe. For the most part, however, the situation today seems to be reversed. An unacknowledged "scientism" – the belief that scientific truth is the only truth – reduces religious truth to the status of feeling, opinion, imagination or downright pathology. At best, it is a matter of faith that lacks any kind of rational support. In Chapter 2 this question was posed: Apart from the question of the truth of Christianity, does Christianity "work" in the sense of satisfying human spiritual needs? Believers might reply that it does so more satisfactorily than do "secular" forms of spirituality. They might further point out that the relationship with a transcendent God fulfills the spiritual need for ultimacy in a more satisfactory way. Non-believers, however, may well reply that belief in a divine, transcendent being is a matter of faith (perhaps even superstition) unsupported by genuine experience or scientific evidence. In other words, the believers' God is not an objective reality but a product of human imagination. In such a case, the human and scientific mentalities cannot find a common ground. Is there any way out of this impasse between science and religion?

In dealing with this problem, the Protestant theologian Paul Tillich poses this question: Is religion a creation of the human spirit or a gift of divine revelation?[14] In other words, is religion a human invention or does it come from God? He then points out how a theologian and a scientist might both disagree and agree in answering this question: (1) They might disagree in the way they answer the question. The theologian might insist that religion is more than a human invention; it is a gift of God's self-disclosure or revelation. The scientist might argue that religion is not the result of any divine initiative but can be explained in psychological or sociological terms. Freud, for instance, maintained that we invent the God we believe in because of a regressive, neurotic need to have, even in adulthood, a loving, protecting father. For him, religion was the result of a father complex. (2) There is, however, a point of agreement between the scientist and the theologian; it lies in the understanding of God and religion that underlies their respective answers. In all likelihood, both define religion as a relationship to a divine being whose existence the theologian affirms and the scientist denies. The existence of God as a divine or supreme being, however, cannot be proved or disproved, though one may construct arguments for both. To base religion on the dubious existence of such a supreme being is to put religion on a shaky foundation and turn faith into an intellectual conundrum. I suggested at the beginning of this chapter that, however much philosophers like to ask it, the question of the existence of God is not the important *religious* question.

Both the scientist and the theologian and, indeed, all those who argue for or against the existence of God, are, in Tillich's view, missing the point. Why? Because they are not speaking of God as the ultimate reality. To speak of God as the supreme being makes God a being just as every other individual entity is a being. But God is not ultimate reality if he is simply one being among many – however supreme he may be. When we speak of God we must use a philosophical category that goes beyond or transcends that of an individual being. Hence Tillich speaks of God as "being itself" or "the ground of all being." Every individual being is a particular expression of something we may

---

[14] *Theology of Culture* (New York: Oxford, 1964), chap. 1.

call "being itself" or being in general and this is therefore a more ultimate category than "a being." Therefore, it more appropriately describes the nature of God as ultimate reality. If we want to describe God using human language, we must use that philosophical category that describes ultimate reality. God is not a particular being like me; God is being itself, of which I and every other particular being is an expression. Moreover, being itself is not a reality the existence of which we can debate; it is immediately and intuitively experienced. That is why arguments for and against the existence of God miss the point; they are arguments about a reality (a supreme being) which God is not.

To illustrate, suppose that you and I are engaged in a heated debate about which is more beautiful, a rose or a lily. (You might also have to imagine that it is a very slow day.) The very fact that we are arguing such a point proves that we are intuitively aware of something we would call beauty itself. We both assume that all beautiful objects are individual instances or expressions of beauty itself. This is the absolute standard against which we measure the beauty of the rose and the lily. This assumption of the reality of beauty is the premise of our discussion; without it, our argument makes no sense. Again, suppose that our argument is not about the relative beauty of two objects, but about the truth or falsity of a particular statement. In this case, we both assume the reality of truth itself. Otherwise, our argument again does not make sense. At a more fundamental level, the existence of particular, individual beings points to the reality of "being itself." This, Tillich argues, is how, philosophically, we should think of God. Even our arguments about the existence of God as a particular (supreme) being assume the reality of being itself, of which all particular beings – even a supreme being – are expressions. This is what Tillich calls "the God beyond God." God is a reality beyond all images we have of God as supreme being, etc. The idea of God as being itself and ourselves as particular beings who participate in and give expression to being itself is echoed in the words of St. Paul: "It is in him that we live and move and exist" (Acts 17:28). The *Catechism of the Catholic Church* (#34) also describes God in this way when it declares that the world and human beings do not possess within themselves their own origin or final end, but rather "participate in Being itself."

48

In the light of all this, what are we to make of the Christian belief in God as that particular being who is the Father of Jesus Christ? How do we reconcile Tillich's philosophical view of God as the seemingly impersonal "ground of being" with our religious view of the very personal God revealed in Christ? To do so we have to keep in mind the nature of revelation. In God's act of self-revelation he adapts the nature of that revelation to the human condition. God is therefore revealed as a person. This accomplishes two things: (1) It reflects the personal quality of being itself. God is the ground of all beings including personal beings. (2) It accommodates the fact that the human person can normally only relate to God as to another person. Most people would have difficulty praying to being itself! It must be kept in mind, however, that all human images of God, even revealed ones, are precisely that – images or human approximations of a reality that is ultimately a mystery beyond human comprehension. Our belief, then, in God as the Father of Jesus Christ and our own Father (however we may envision that) does not exhaust the meaning of what God is in himself; it is belief in God as he wants to be known to us. The *Catechism of the Catholic Church* (#42) reminds us that all human words and images fail to fully express the nature of God since they "always fall short of the mystery of God." It further warns us not to confuse God with our human representations of God. Many people who reject God are in fact not rejecting God but an image of God passed on to them by their pastors, teachers or parents (or the image they *think* was passed on to them).

What all this amounts to is that we should all be a bit iconoclastic, in the sense that we recognize the inadequacy of human images to convey the full reality of God and the sacred. Catholic tradition, nevertheless, has always upheld the validity of using human words, images and metaphors to represent God. This is based on the idea that there is some kind of analogy between God and humanity, given that we are created in God's image. This means that certain terms can be applied to both God and human beings in somewhat the same way. Thus we can legitimately call God our "Father," even though the reality of God infinitely transcends the meaning of this human term. As philosopher Leszek Kolakowski has observed, Christians "have never given up the belief that God is both Father and the

Absolute."[15] In other words, Christians find no incongruity in thinking of God as the absolute, infinite, "impersonal" ground of being, while at the same time thinking of God as a particular being, a benevolent father who cares not only for all his children, but for each of them separately. The former is a *philosophical* way of trying to express the essence of God, to describe what God is in himself. The latter is a *religious* way of relating to that same God as he has revealed himself to us, as he wants to be known to us. Is it not the same with our human relationships? I can become friends with another only insofar as we both open up and reveal something of ourselves to each other. We both know that there is more to the other than our friendship reveals, but this does not undermine our friendship. Nor is our friendship with God undermined because the image by which we know him does not reveal his full reality. The religious question about God is not the philosophical question. It is not "What is God in himself?" It is rather "What is God to me?" Christians believe that this religious question is answered in the person of Jesus Christ, in whom the divine nature is humanly expressed. God must have known that most of us are not philosophers!

We are left with the question of the adequacy of the image of God as our Father. Does it adequately answer the religious question and fulfill our religious needs? In our own times some Christian feminists have raised the question of whether the Christian image of God is one-sidedly masculine or "patriarchal." Does this image adequately reflect the fact that all of us – male and female – are created in God's image? For some who feel strongly about this issue, there may be no adequate answer. Nevertheless, the following two points, I believe, should be kept in mind in discussing this question: (1) The fact that God is revealed to us as Father does not mean that God is exclusively "masculine," or that only those who are masculine reflect God's image. Since God is beyond gender, the so-called masculine image must be seen against the background of the creation story. "God created man in the image of himself, in the image of God he created him, male and female he created them"

---

[15] *Religion: On God, the Devil, Sin and other Worries of the So-called Philosophy of Religion* (London: Fontana, 1993), p. 141.

(Genesis 1:27). Obviously, then, male and female *together* constitute a totality that reflects the image of God. In isolation neither is a complete expression of the divine image. Both together are required to express that human totality that reflects the image of God. (2) Every parent knows that being a good father means more than being a man and that being a good mother means more than being a woman. A good father must also have "motherly" qualities, just as a good mother must have "fatherly" qualities. It would be a mistake to think of God our Father as exclusively masculine.

Jesus who, according to our faith, is God incarnate, certainly exhibited the "feminine" virtues of tenderness and compassion, especially in his attitude to children, sinners, the marginalized members of society and those "who labour and are overburdened" (Matthew 11:28). His concern for his own people is described as a motherly one: "How often have I longed to gather your children, as a hen gathers her chicks under her wings" (Matthew 23:37). The prophet Isaiah uses a similar mother image to describe the love of God for his people: "At her breast will her nurslings be carried and fondled in her lap. Like a son comforted by his mother will I comfort you" (Isaiah 66:12-13). Andrew Greeley, commenting on this kind of imagery, writes: "Is God really like a fair bride? Does she really care for us like a mother who has brought us into the world? Does she really nurse us at the breast? Does she really seduce us like an attractive lover who has determined to make us Her own? How can anyone who is Catholic say 'No'?"[16]

Greeley's concluding question suggests that it is almost unthinkable for a Catholic to have a one-sidedly masculine understanding of God. Where God is understood as a father, there must be compensating images to express the "feminine," motherly aspect of God. For Catholic tradition, these complementary images are found principally in its understanding of the role of the Church ("Mother Church") and most particularly in the cult of the Virgin Mary. In another place, Greeley points out that the Virgin Mary's role within

---

[16] Andrew Greeley and Mary Greeley Durkin, *How to Save the Catholic Church* (New York: Viking Penguin, 1984), p. 151.

Christianity is analogous to that of the goddesses of ancient religions; she reflects the feminine aspect of God.[17] It is curious that, at a time when this kind of balancing and compensating imagery is sorely needed, both the nurturing role of the Church and the role of Mary in Catholic life seem to be less of a focus than ever.

---

[17] *The Great Mysteries* (New York: Seabury, 1976), p. 119.

## PART II

## THE MEANING OF FAITH

For Christians, the experience of grace and faith is the fundamental religious experience. If grace is the love of God, faith is the response to that love. For the Christian, faith means to accept and believe in God's love as revealed in the person of Jesus Christ. As with belief in and response to anyone's love, it engages more than the mind; it involves more than believing doctrines about God. In this section we will explore the meaning of faith. What we want to understand is this:

1) What are the elements that make up our response to God that we call faith?

2) What are the stages by which our faith develops?

3) How are we changed or transformed or "reborn" by our experience of grace and faith?

## 4. WHAT IS FAITH?

If there is a single underlying premise to this book, it is the conviction that a fundamental misunderstanding of the meaning of faith is at the root of the perplexed Catholic's distorted understanding of the Christian tradition. In Chapter 3 we spoke of the historical process that led to a certain "intellectualizing" of the meaning of faith. Among Catholics there is still a tendency to limit the understanding of faith to faith as belief, the assent of one's mind to doctrines taught by the Church. Perhaps we were taught as children that faith meant believing certain truths that were revealed by God and proposed for our belief by the Church. (Recall the "act of faith" you were taught to recite.) No doubt those who instilled this understanding of faith in us believed that they were being consistent with the teaching of St. Thomas Aquinas, who defined faith as "The act of the intellect when it assents to divine truth, under the influence of the will moved by God through grace."[18] Even as it stands, this definition conveys a rather intellectualized understanding of faith. It is an "act of the intellect." It becomes even more so when a tradition emphasizes the intellect's "assent to truth," while leaving the words "moved by God through grace" relatively underdeveloped. The result was the notion that faith meant assent to the teachings of the Church. The action of God's grace was seen as referring to the fact that, in some mysterious way, faith was a "gift of God." Those who lament their "lack of faith" because they struggle with this truncated understanding of faith may have more faith than they imagine.

None of the above is intended to deny that belief is an important element of our faith. There is a difference, however, between believing truths about God and believing *in* God. To illustrate this difference, compare these two different statements. Suppose your high school history teacher informed you that the Battle of Hastings was fought in the year 1066. You take down the information, commit it to memory and reproduce it on a test, to the satisfaction of all concerned. In doing so, you have

---

[18] *Summa Theologiae,* Part 2-2, Question 2, article 9.

shown "faith" in your teacher, in that you believe the information he or she gives you as true and you trust that he or she is not deceiving you. If the information should turn out to be incorrect, you may question the teacher's competence, but you are not upset in a deeply personal way. You can always look up the correct information. Your trust is not shattered, nor do you feel personally betrayed, because the information imparted was an objective piece of information, the truth or falsity of which is independent of your personal relationship with the teacher. Now, by way of contrast, suppose that the man or woman of your dreams says to you, "I love you," and you believe it. Once again, you have shown faith in another, but as we all know, it is a very different kind of faith. This kind of faith demands a much more profound level of trust. We are not dealing, in this instance, with communicating an objective piece of information. The other is communicating his or her deepest feelings towards you – not just factual information, but subjective feelings. Trusting that the other is not deceiving you now carries a much greater risk. In this act of faith, trust plays a far more fundamental role since you have a far more personal stake in what the other is saying and in your response. You not only trust the other's honesty and integrity but, as it were, entrust yourself to it.

When we say that this kind of trust is the most fundamental element in the faith of the Christian, it is because that faith (as we saw in Chapter 2) is a response to God's statement "I love you," spoken to all of us collectively and to each one of us individually. When we speak of "believing in" another, we emphasize this element of trust. One of the concerns of the Protestant reformers was to reaffirm this element of trust in Christian faith, to emphasize that faith means believing *in* God and not merely believing truths *about* God. Compare, for instance, Thomas Aquinas' definition of faith given above with this description of faith given by Martin Luther:

> There are two ways of believing. The first consists of believing of God, that is, believing as true what is said of God.... The other way is to believe in God; not only do I believe as true

what is said of God, but I place my trust in him, I believe without doubt that he will be and will act with me according to what is said of him.... Only a faith which trusts absolutely in God, in life and unto death makes the Christian and obtains all from God.... This little word "in" is so true. Observe that we do not say, "I believe God the Father" or "of God the Father" but in God the Father, in Jesus Christ, and this fact is due to God alone.[19]

When Luther wrote these words he was convinced that, far from preaching a new doctrine, he was reaffirming the teaching of St. Paul. The object of Christian faith is a God who, in the person of Jesus Christ, proclaims his love and acceptance of all of us and promises us eternal life. The individual Christian can experience the transforming power of that love and its culmination in eternal life (that is, can experience salvation) only through faith, through a trusting belief in God's love and promise. The love of another person has no effect on me unless I accept it and believe in it, unless I have *faith* in the other. Luther was stressing this indispensable role of faith when he said that we are saved *sola fide* (by faith alone). God's declaration of love for us requires more than intellectual assent. It cannot be treated like a piece of objective information such as one might hear on the evening news. Like any declaration of love, it requires faith *in* the person who offers it. The proper response is the response of the whole person, not just the assent of the mind.

Luther's teaching on this point is rejected by those who think of faith as mere belief in a set of doctrines since, in their minds, it raises this question: How can intellectual assent to doctrines bring about one's salvation, since intellectual beliefs can remain unrelated to and exercise little transforming power on one's life? Is it not also necessary to live a good life? Did not the apostle James teach that faith without "good works" is dead? (James 2:17). But neither Luther nor St. Paul nor St. James understood faith merely as orthodox belief. They understood faith as a trusting belief in and acceptance of God's redeeming

---

[19] "Eine kurze Form des Glaubens," quoted in Mark Link (ed.), *Faith and Commitment* (Chicago: Loyola University Press, 1964), p. 108.

love. This kind of faith has the potential to transform a person just as human love does. One's life then becomes a grateful response to God's gift of love and acceptance. This, in turn, is the kind of life that produces "good works," which are the spontaneous consequence of genuine faith and not a means of earning one's salvation. Is it not a fact of human experience that love changes us and changes the way we live? It seems, therefore, that we misinterpret St. James when we understand him to say that good works must be added to our faith in order to ensure our salvation. His emphasis seems rather to be on the quality of our faith. A faith, he maintains, that does not spontaneously produce a good life and good works, that allows us to be indifferent to the real needs of our neighbours, is not a genuine faith; it is "quite dead." Good works are to be seen as evidence of genuine faith – a faith that saves. To use Luther's analogy, the fruit does not make the tree good; the tree makes the fruit good. Genuine faith is the tree that produces the fruit of a morally good life.

Faith, then, must include not only belief (assent to doctrine) but also a trusting acceptance of God's revealed love. I have also suggested that it is inseparable from "good works" or moral commitment. These three elements – belief, trust and moral commitment – make up the total personal response of the Christian believer to God's act of self-revelation in Christ. It is to this total personal response to God's love or grace that we give the name *faith*. Traditional Christian doctrine speaks of our trusting belief (faith) in God's freely given, redemptive love (grace) as the source of our "justification" or "righteousness." It is probably better to avoid these traditional terms, since they have connotations that tend to turn them into the opposite of their intended meaning. Even when that intended meaning has been made clear, it is still difficult to hear these words without translating them into "self-justification" and "self-righteousness." Both carry a suggestion of smug satisfaction with one's virtue or accomplishments. Of course, there is usually a feeling of satisfaction when one has completed a task or acted dutifully. The Christian teaching, however, is that our "righteousness" – our acceptability before God – is not grounded in our human accomplishments but in the grace of God. Perhaps we should understand both these terms, then, as referring to the experience of a right relationship with God, to the assurance of God's love and acceptance.

The Christian doctrine of "justification through faith," then, refers to the fact that God's loving acceptance cannot be earned or merited; as a freely given gift, it can only be accepted in faith. To use Tillich's phrase, faith is "accepting acceptance" – accepting the fact that we are accepted by God. It is for this reason that the Church has always looked to the biblical patriarch Abraham as the prototype and exemplar of faith. He is the "father of believers" because, as with the Christian believer, his faith and not any human accomplishment is the basis for his justifying relationship with God. The biblical story of Abraham (Genesis 12–25) begins with God's summoning Abraham to leave his homeland and his kinfolk and to go "to the land I will show you." At the same time, God promises Abraham – in his old age – that he will have a son and, through that son, countless descendants. Abraham, according to the biblical account, "put his trust in the LORD, who counted this as making him justified" (Genesis 15:6). St. Paul points out that Abraham was not justified before God because he observed God's law, but simply because he had faith in God's promise. In the same way, the Christian is not justified by successfully observing God's law, but by believing in God's love and promise. Therefore, "it is those who rely on faith who are the sons of Abraham" and "receive the same blessing as Abraham, the man of faith" (Galatians 3:6-9).

Abraham is the father of believers, in the sense that those who imitate his faith are his spiritual descendants. After noting that Abraham was justified by his faith, Pope St. Clement I comments: "We too, whom God has called in Christ Jesus, are justified, not by our own efforts – our wisdom or understanding or piety or good deeds – but by faith, through which God has justified men from the beginning."[20] In short, we do not earn God's love; we believe he loves us because he said so. We do not earn eternal life; we expect it because God has promised it. Pope Clement I, the third successor of St. Peter, lived in the first century. This is clearly the teaching of the Church from the

---

[20] *Letter to the Corinthians*, 32:4.

earliest times; and yet it seems to run contrary to the deeply ingrained legalistic attitudes of many Christians.

Abraham's faith experience, when seen in the context of the biblical account, is prototypical of all the biblical stories of encounters between God and his people. It must be kept in mind that Abraham's faith is a response to God's intervention in his life. This seems to be characteristic of the biblical view of God's relationship with his people. Nothing happens until God takes the initiative. God "speaks" in some way to an individual or to the community through a prophet. This speaking takes the form of a call to some task or destiny. Associated with this call is a promise – usually a promise that contradicts all human expectation. The human response to God's call and promise is faith. The result of this divine initiative and human response of faith is a new relationship with God which, in biblical terms, is called a "covenant." In the biblical view, then, the divine/human encounter seems to follow this three stage dynamic: (1) divine call and promise; (2) the human response (faith); (3) a new relationship or covenant.

In Abraham's case, the call of God is a call to leave his family and homeland and to go to "the land I will show you." In return, God makes a preposterous promise to the 75-year-old Abraham and his 65-year-old wife, Sarah: though they have been childless all these years, they will have a son and descendants and that Abraham would thereby be the father of a great nation (Genesis 12:1-3). Furthermore, the promise is not fulfilled until Abraham is 100 and Sarah is 90! Biblical scholars might caution us not to take these numbers too literally. However, the intent of the biblical author is clear: to emphasize that Abraham puts his faith in a promise that contradicts all human wisdom and all human expectation. In the same way, a motley crew of refugee slaves led by Moses puts its faith in a promise of a land of their own, and the Christian believer puts his or her faith in the promise of eternal life.

In Abraham's faith response to God's call and promise we can find, I believe, the three essential elements of faith – belief, trust and commitment. There may seem to be little in the way of intellectual belief in Abraham's faith. God simply calls him and he responds with action: "So Abraham went as the LORD told him" (Genesis 12:4). And yet in that action there is surely an implicit belief in the reality of the God who speaks to him. Abraham obviously did not believe that his religious experience was a delusion or a projection of his own psychological needs or a merely naturalistic "peak experience." The God who spoke to him was, in Abraham's mind, real. This is belief.

The formal element of Abraham's faith, that which truly makes it faith, is the element of trust. In going "as the LORD told him," he gives up all his human sources of security. He leaves behind his kinfolk, homeland, property, etc., and entrusts his future security and happiness to God. Furthermore, as we have seen, he puts his trust in a promise that is contrary to human experience and expectation. His trust is further put to the test by the fact that he must wait another 25 years for the promise to be fulfilled. During this time he loses patience and tries to bring about the fulfillment of the promise through his own human ingenuity (Genesis 16). He takes Sarah's maidservant Hagar as his mistress. However, the child born of this union (Ishmael) is rejected by God as the son of the promise. God reiterates that Sarah will bear a son as promised. The point seems to be that Abraham's reliance on his own human resources rather than God's promise is a failure of faith. It also suggests that faith is a fragile possession that must be constantly reaffirmed.

Moral commitment is also an integral part of Abraham's faith response to God's call and promise. This commitment takes the form of fidelity to the covenant that God establishes between himself and Abraham and his descendants. In a passage (Genesis 15) that is strange to our ears, God inaugurates this covenant. He commands Abraham to take a number of animals, cut them in half and arrange the halves in two lines facing each other. God then passes between the divided animals in the form of smoke and fire and repeats his promise: "To your descendants I give this land, from the wadi of Egypt to the Great River" (Genesis 15:18). Biblical scholars suggest that this was an ancient ritual used to enter into a formal contract or covenant. Both parties would pass between the divided animals as if to say, "May I meet the fate of these animals if I fail to keep the terms of this covenant." Notice, however, that in this case only God passes between the animals. He acts unilaterally. Abraham can respond only with faith. But faith has moral consequences that, for Abraham, take the form of a readiness to do what God expects of him. The entrusting of one's security, happiness and fulfillment to God that faith implies carries with it, as a natural consequence, a surrender of one's own will to the will of God. This is the lesson that Abraham learned the hard way in his experience with Hagar and Ishmael. Christian faith also implies a surrender to the will of God. This becomes the ultimate guideline for one's life and the ultimate criterion for moral decision-making.

In the faith experience of the Christian believer, a similar dynamic can be observed. God calls us to life in Christ and promises eternal life. In our human faith response to that call and promise, the element of belief is much more explicit than in the case of Abraham. Our encounter with God is not immediate and direct but mediated by the teachings of the Church (including the Scriptures). These teachings announce and elaborate on the Christian message of salvation. The assent to basic doctrines, then, seems to be an essential first step in our experience of faith. Trust, however, remains the primary and formal element of faith. The believer puts his trust not in his ability to earn God's love and eternal life through his own human resources, but in God's declaration of his love and his promise of eternal life. Also, as with Abraham, our faith implies a moral commitment, because God's call and promise and our faith response bring about a new relationship or covenant (a new "testament") between God and us. In this case, however, it is not a formal contract as with Abraham; it is a personal relationship that makes us "children of God." God, who wants to be our Father, calls us to be his children and thereby share in Christ's relationship with the Father. Hence we live "in Christ." Our moral commitment is to the obligations inherent in that personal relationship; we are called to live as children of God. All the Church's moral teachings are intended to facilitate that fundamental commitment.

The act and commitment of faith is sometimes called a "leap of faith." This is not because faith is something compulsive or irrational; it is because faith is a radical act of trust and therefore involves the acceptance of risk and insecurity. To put my trust and find my security in God means that, to some extent, I give up my human sources of security and confidence. Sometimes this may involve giving up material sources of security, as Abraham did when he gave up family and homeland and property and set off on his seemingly madcap adventure. At other times, it might mean giving up reliance on our human wisdom and ingenuity. Abraham's faith faltered when he tried (with Hagar's help) to produce through his own human efforts the child promised by God rather than trusting in God's promise. This does not mean that we are to give up the responsibility to think and act for ourselves in confronting life's problems; it does mean that some problems require more than human know-how. The sixth-century Irish monk St. Columban reminds us that faith, and the transformation it effects, brings with it a wisdom that is superior to human wisdom: "Seek the highest knowledge, therefore, not in wordy argument but in integrity of life; not through words but through faith that arises from simplicity of heart and not from the conjectures of learned fools. If you seek the ineffable One in human books, he will recede from you further than before; if you seek him through faith, he will abide where he is – at the gates of wisdom, where he abides and may be partially seen."[21] This kind of language reminds us that faith transforms one's values, radically alters one's perspective and therefore imparts a deeper kind of wisdom.

Most essentially, Christian faith involves giving up reliance on our own human goodness, on the conviction that our virtue or piety or good life is sufficient to earn God's love and acceptance. Legalists insist on trying to earn, through observance of moral laws, something that they have already been freely given. Why? Because they want the *security* of knowing that they have earned God's love and acceptance; the security of knowing that God "owes" them, because they have kept God's law perfectly. People of faith, on the other hand, must abandon this kind of security. They know that love cannot be earned; their confidence in God's love comes from God's assurance, not from their own human efforts. This does not mean that their moral effort is any less than that of the legalists; it means that

---

[21] *Instructions on the Faith,* Instruction 1, no. 5.

God's love is the cause, not the result, of their moral effort. God does not love them because they are good; they are good because God loves them.

The *Catechism of the Catholic Church* (#1994) refers to our justification before God as "the most excellent work of God's love." We enjoy God's love simply because God gratuitously loves and accepts us, not because we have earned it in any way. This does not mean that there is no point to our efforts to live a good moral life. Catholic tradition has always emphasized that the process of our salvation includes both the grace of *justification* (God's act of love and acceptance) to which we respond by faith, and the ongoing process of *sanctification* (the process of overcoming the alienating effects of sin and living as children of God). This is the work of the Holy Spirit; our moral effort is our co-operation in that work. It reminds us that God's call and promise is more than a comforting assurance of God's love and acceptance. It is a call to moral conversion, to live as children whom God loves and in whose image we are created. St. Columban describes the goal of sanctification as returning to God the image in which God created us and adds: "Let us not paint an alien image in ourselves; the painter who is undisciplined, angry and proud paints the picture of a tyrant. Therefore, lest we end with a self-portrait of a despot, let us allow Christ to paint his image in us."[22] The moral life is an attempt to live up to the dignity that is already ours; it is not an attempt to earn a reward.

Sometimes people ask: Why do some people have faith and others do not? The glib answer is that faith is a gift of God. This is a puzzling answer and, quite frankly, a little too Calvinistic to sound like Catholic teaching. Does it imply that God gives faith (and all its benefits) to some and not to others? Does God play favourites? Are we either among the "elect" or the "reprobate"? What does it say about an individual's freedom of choice? Does it happen to us whether we want it or not? The *Catechism of the Catholic Church* (#160) seems to reject such thinking when it asserts that "to be human, [our] response to God must be free." In what sense, then, is faith a gift? The confusion arises, I believe, when we mistake our response to the

---

[22] *Instructions on the Faith,* Instruction 11, no. 2.

gift for the gift itself. If someone offers me a gift, it remains useless and ineffective unless I accept it and use it. Faith is the acceptance and use of the gift of God's grace, of God's freely given love. But even the love of God is useless and ineffective unless the recipient accepts it, believes in it and acts on it. Grace, then – not faith – is the gift; faith is our acceptance of that gift. Faith is a gift only in the sense that it does not happen apart from the gift of grace – a gift that is offered to everyone. This of course does not resolve the issue of why some people respond to the gift and others do not, an issue that is both theological and psychological. The modest purpose of this discussion is simply to make a little sense out of a piece of Catholic tradition as most of us remember it.

# 5. HOW DOES FAITH HAPPEN?

In Chapter 4, we raised a question: Why do some people respond to the revelation of God's love while others do not? The answer to this question is ultimately a mystery, since the reasons are so complex. At the same time we should note that our human experience poses the same question. Why do some people respond positively to the love of others while many find it difficult, if not impossible, to accept love? Furthermore, we must keep in mind that we cannot simply identify those who have faith with Christian believers or even only with those who have some kind of explicitly religious faith. The experience of faith is more extensive than its religious expression. As Paul Tillich puts it: "Grace can happen in many ways. It does not need religion. God does not make grace dependent on the existence of religion."[23] Perhaps the only question we can fruitfully explore is this: Among those who have faith, how does that faith come about or develop? This leads to other questions: Can we trace a pattern of development, a dynamic or series of stages one passes through in one's growth towards authentic faith? Can we say that our faith development follows the three-stage pattern of childhood, adolescence and adulthood, just as our human development does? In what sense does faith represent a stage of religious adulthood? I believe that St. Paul answers this question. Before turning to St. Paul, we should recall the meaning of these three stages in the context of our human growth.

I believe we can characterize these three stages psychologically, in terms of a person's growing self-awareness, as follows. (1) *Infancy and childhood* represent a state of "unself-consciousness." The infant and toddler have not yet developed an inner sense of personal identity, are not yet fully conscious of self. Hence the lack of a fully developed sense of moral responsibility (conscience). The child at this stage is not self-reflective but "outer directed," fully occupied with discovering his or her environment. As every parent knows, this curiosity is

---

[23] *The Irrelevance and Relevance of Religion* (Cleveland: Pilgrim Press, 1996), p. 56.

so great that it requires "child-proof" kitchens and safety locks on car doors. (2) *Adolescence* represents the apex of one's growing sense of "self-consciousness." This growing self-awareness finds expression as a preoccupation with one's inner sense of identity, one's abilities, one's future role in the world, one's present popularity, acceptability to peers, etc. The adolescent is definitely "inner directed" or preoccupied with himself or herself. The desire to be "cool," to conform to current standards of dress and hairstyles and ways of talking, are superficial expressions of a deeper desire to be a worthwhile and acceptable person. Acceptable to whom? To oneself, to others and – if the adolescent is religious – to God. (3) *Adulthood* is characterized by the overcoming (transcending) of adolescent self-preoccupation. To be an adult means that the adolescent problems of self-identity and self-worth have been sufficiently resolved that one can assume the "outer directed" responsibilities of adulthood: work to do, people to love, children to raise, problems to solve. Adulthood implies a certain capacity for "self-forgetfulness." The adult has achieved sufficient self-acceptance to be able to "forget" herself or himself in commitment to others and the world. It is, in a sense, a recapturing of the outer directedness of the child, but without the child's lack of self-awareness. Thus Jesus did not tell us to remain children, but to "change and become like little children" (Matthew 18:3). Being a mature Christian is incompatible with adolescent self-preoccupation; it requires self-forgetfulness.

If we reflect on certain passages in the writings of St. Paul – particularly in Romans and Galatians – the following points, I believe, will be made clear: (1) Faith is, for the Christian, the fundamental religious experience and, therefore, the foundation of the Christian life. (2) Faith, as a state of religious maturity, has the same characteristics as human psychological maturity. (3) We grow towards faith or religious maturity in a way that is analogous to human growth, by passing through those three stages of growth that we have described as states of unself-consciousness, self-consciousness and self-forgetfulness. Though he does not use these terms, it is clear that St. Paul sees the faith by which he responds to God's self-revelation in Christ as a state of religious adulthood. It represents the culmination of a process that includes, as a necessary prelude, stages of religious childhood and adolescence. Paul's language is that of a first-century Jewish convert to Christianity. Using the three stages of Judeo-Christian religious history as an analogy, he describes the three stages of faith development as living without law, living under the law and living (by faith) under grace. Since these passages are letters and not theological treatises, Paul's presentation is not systematic. Nevertheless, it seems clear that he sees his own spiritual journey towards faith (and, by implication, that of every Christian believer) as an experience of these three stages.

1. *Living without law.* This phrase describes the religious childhood both of humanity and of the individual. Paul compares it to the religious state of those who lived "from Adam to Moses." It is a time when people lived without the law to the extent that God's law – which appeared only with Moses – had not yet been revealed. The fact that there was no divine law to transgress did not mean that there was no such thing as sin, however. Sin, as already noted, is the state of alienation and separation that is part of the human condition. Thus Paul says, "Sin existed in the world long before the law was given. There was no law and so no one could be accused of the sin of 'law-breaking' " (Romans 5:13). When the law of Moses (which includes the Ten Commandments) appears, it does not suddenly invent sin, for sin is already an aspect of the human condition. What does it do, then? It presents people with a moral ideal to live up to. When they fail, when they transgress the law, it makes them aware of the egoism deeply rooted in their human nature, which is at the heart of that state of separation and alienation we have called sin. In other words, the law makes people aware of the state of sin in which they exist; it becomes the occasion for the experience of guilt. Without the law, people lived in a state of childlike unself-consciousness, unaware of their sin and guilt.

In the life cycle of the individual, infancy and early childhood is the unself-conscious period of living without law. It is the period before the development of conscience and commitment to moral values. Because of this, it is a state of illusion and ignorance. In this stage, I am unaware of my real condition, unaware that my egoistic and self-centred behaviour has any moral quality. The toddler might feel fear of punishment for his or her destructive behaviour but does not feel inner guilt; nor does the parent ascribe any moral culpability to this phase of childhood. It is a time of "innocence" since it precedes any awareness of moral laws and, therefore, of moral guilt. Sometimes we tend to wax nostalgic about this state of innocence and regret its loss. Yet in the interests of becoming fully human it must be outgrown. Full human development requires growth in self-awareness with the accompanying development of conscience and moral responsibility. With this comes the capacity for experiencing guilt. Like Adam and Eve we "fall" from the paradise of childhood innocence. And like Adam and Eve, who were barred from re-entering the garden by an angel with a flaming sword, we cannot return to it. Guilt is not something foisted on the world by religion. The ability to experience guilt is a necessary part of our humanness.

2. *Living under the law.* Paul likens this transition from "innocence" to an awareness of sin and guilt to the religious situation of those who lived "under the law," from the time of Moses to the coming of Christ. It is only with the giving of the law through Moses that people become more acutely aware of sin and guilt through their failure to live up to the law's moral demands. Thus begins the period of adolescent self-consciousness in the religious history of humankind. Trying to live up to the demands of the moral law serves to remind us of our moral inadequacy: hence the experience of sin and guilt. Paul's use of the period "from Moses to Christ" to illustrate this stage of "living under the law" should not be understood as dismissing the Judaism of that period as nothing but a religion of law. This was also the time of the great prophets who reminded the people that there was more to religion than observance of laws. Jews, Christians and religious people of all stripes have been guilty of distorting religion by turning the law into a means of earning God's love and acceptance. Our efforts to observe the law – even God's law – are inadequate only in reference to their ability to "justify" us before God. We cannot earn God's love by keeping God's law; our failed efforts to observe that law perfectly are intended to convince us of that fact. As long as we cling to the illusion that God's favour can be earned by scrupulous moral and religious observance, we remain impervious to God's offer of his freely given love, of his grace. As Paul says to the

Galatians: "If you look to the law to make you justified, then you have separated yourselves from Christ, and have fallen from grace" (Galatians 5:4).

Paul describes his own transition from living without law to living under the law as follows: "Once when there was no law, I was alive; but when the commandment came, sin came to life and I died" (Romans 7:9-10). Ignorant of sin and guilt, he has the illusion of being "alive." This illusion gives way to a death-like experience of sin and guilt when he encounters the moral law and tries to live up to its demands. This leads him to ask whether the moral law is therefore something evil in that it robs him of "life," of his unself-conscious state of "innocence." This is an idea he emphatically rejects: "The law is sacred and what it commands is sacred, just and good. Does that mean that something good killed me? Of course not. But sin, to show itself in its true colours, used that good thing to kill me; and thus sin, thanks to the commandment, was able to exercise all its sinful power" (Romans 7:12-13). Here Paul makes two important points: (1) In itself the moral law is good in that it confronts us with valid moral principles that we must pursue in order to be fully human; (2) While the law is good in itself, it becomes not the cause but the occasion for guilt, frustration and anxiety (Paul's "death") that we experience when we fail to justify ourselves by perfectly fulfilling its demands. The real culprit in this scenario is not the law but sin or egoism, which frustrates our attempts at self-justification. The whole experience leads to an awareness of sin "in its true colours" and to the conclusion that God's acceptance of us cannot be earned by living a morally and religiously perfect life. In other words, we need redemption or grace.

This experience of living "under the law" seems to be a necessary preliminary to the experience of grace and faith, just as in our human development adolescence is a necessary preliminary to adulthood. Looking at only one aspect of this question, we can say that the adolescent is an idealist; he pursues an ideal image. To bolster his fragile sense of identity, he tries to live up to this idealized image of himself. In this way he tries to feel good about himself, be popular and well-liked among his peers and, if he is religious, to win God's approval. In other words, he is trying to "justify" himself, render himself worthy and acceptable by his own human efforts. In order for him to become an adult, this idealism has to fail; not in the sense that he must stop trying to become his ideal self, but in the sense that he must realize that all his efforts to do so will never command the love and acceptance of others. When he comes to the realization that he is loved and accepted by those closest to him without having to earn it – without having to perfectly fulfill his self ideal – he is liberated from the pressure of constantly having to prove or justify himself. He is then able to outgrow his adolescent preoccupation with his identity, self-worth, etc. He is now able to stop worrying about himself – to 'forget" himself – to a degree that allows him to assume those outer directed concerns we have associated with adulthood. He may not use the word, but he has experienced "grace."

In the process of faith development, a similar transition from religious adolescence to religious adulthood takes place. To live "under the law" means to attempt to justify or render oneself worthy and acceptable before God through one's human efforts, through one's moral and religious accomplishments. This tends to promote a legalistic type of religious observance in which everything depends on one's success or failure in living up to the demands of what is perceived as God's law. Small wonder that this is sometimes referred to as the "oppression" of the law. God is seen as lawgiver. He has imposed his law on us as an oppressive burden. We earn his promised rewards by living up to the demands of this law. This is such a complete distortion of the Christian message as to be heretical. In fact, this kind of thinking, in the form of "Pelagianism," was condemned as heretical by the Church in the fifth century. Nevertheless it seems to form the basis of the religious life of many Christians. Perhaps it is the only version of the Christian message they have been taught. As with the adolescent, the transition from "living under the law" to "living under grace" is the result of a twofold realization: (1) It is impossible to perfectly fulfill the demands of the moral law and, even if one could do so, one would fall short of earning God's love since love cannot be earned; (2) What one has been trying to earn or be worthy of has in fact been given freely and unconditionally, without the condition of one's being worthy or deserving of it. This is grace and it happens only when we abandon the project of justifying ourselves.

In a classic passage in his letter to the Romans, St. Paul describes his experience of living under the law as a process fraught with guilt, anxiety and frustration. Here is what happens, he seems to be saying, when an individual, sharing in the human condition of sin, encounters the moral law and tries to live up to its demands.

> The Law of course, as we all know, is spiritual; but I am unspiritual; I have been sold as a slave to sin. I cannot understand my own behaviour. I fail to carry out the things I want to do, and I find myself doing the very things I hate. When I act against my own will, that means I have a self that acknowledges that the Law is good, and so the thing behaving in that way is not myself but the sin living in me. The fact is, I know of nothing good living in me – living, that is, in my unspiritual self – for though the will to do what is good is in me, the performance is not, with the result that, instead of doing the good things I want to do, I carry out the sinful things I do not want. When I act against my will, then, it is not my true self doing it, but sin which lives in me. In fact, this seems to be the rule, that every single time I want to do good it is something evil that comes to hand. In my inmost self I dearly love God's law, but I can see that my body follows a different law that battles against the law which my reason dictates. This is what makes me a prisoner of that law of sin which lives inside my body. What a wretched man I am! Who will rescue me from this body doomed to death? Thanks be to God through Jesus Christ our Lord! (Romans 7:12-25)

Who among us cannot identify with this experience, even though our own experience may not be as traumatic as Paul's? It is the age-old problem of the mystery of evil; the conflict between my knowledge of the good to be done and the inability of my will to carry it out; the conflict between the person I ought and want to be (my ideal self) and the person I actually am (my actual self). The result is that I do what my better judgment tells me not to do and fail to do what reason dictates I should do.

It is interesting that when former U.S. president Bill Clinton admitted to an improper sexual relationship with a White House intern, he described his behaviour as an "error in judgment." Is it not more likely that the president's judgment about the appropriateness of what he was doing was in fact quite sound? The problem more likely seems to be that he was unable to resist the impulse to act against his better judgment. But what is it that makes us act in this contradictory way? Paul's answer is unequivocal. It is "sin living within me." We have described sin as the unredeemed human condition, the condition of alienation or separation from self, others and God or what is ultimate in the scale of things. In this instance, Paul experiences it as self-alienation, the separation between what he wants to be and what he actually is. Sin – in the sense of original sin – is what makes it impossible for us to realize our full human potential. So great is its effect that, even though it is an aspect of his human nature, Paul speaks of it as if it were an alien power. When he does what is evil against his better judgment, he seems to say, it is not "the real me," not the self that deep down dearly loves God's law. It is sin that makes him follow a different law.

The experience that St. Paul describes in the above passage is what Christian tradition came to refer to as the "bondage of the will." Sin holds the human will, as it were, in a state of bondage or slavery by impelling us to act against our better judgment. If sin is the human state of separation, its consequence is a fundamental egoism that is rooted in our human nature. Lacking genuine relatedness to others, to God and even to my own deepest self, the isolated ego becomes the centre of my concern. I believe that our human experience verifies the proposition that every sin, in the sense of a transgression of the moral law, is an expression of that egoism that undermines our best intentions. When we make choices, we do so freely, but because of the reality of sin or egoism, we do not always choose rightly or wisely. We sometimes choose selfishly, that is, sinfully. The Christian doctrine of sin as expressed in Church teaching or mythically in the biblical story of Adam and Eve has had to reconcile these two aspects. Sin is both inevitable and, therefore, seemingly involuntary and, at the same time, freely chosen. What is a hard nut for logic to crack is affirmed by our human experience. Despite all the blather about "a firm purpose of amendment," no Catholics leaving the confessional really believe they will never sin again; but they also know that, when they do, they will do so freely.

Here, then, is the situation of the religious person seeking a justifying relationship with God. She tries to win God's love and approval by keeping what she perceives to be God's law. She discovers that this is impossible, because she is unable to keep God's law perfectly. Through her transgressions of the law, she comes to the same realization as did St. Paul: the source of her transgressions against the law is an aspect of her human nature that makes her act contrary to her good intentions. This is what Paul calls sin. This awareness of sin and the resulting experience of guilt bring her attempts to earn God's approval to a dead end. At the same time, her failure to justify herself – to prove herself worthy – creates in her a readiness to receive God's love and acceptance as a free gift: to accept grace. This accepting of God's grace is faith.

3. *Living under grace*. In the context of our growth towards religious maturity or faith, living "under the law" serves a threefold purpose. First, the attempt to earn God's approval through our own human efforts brings us – through our failure to do so – to an awareness of sin and guilt: the sinful condition of separation and egoism that is at the root of all our transgressions of the moral law. Second, this painful awareness of sin and guilt leads us to an awareness of our need for redemption. We are aware that we cannot earn God's love, not only because of the inadequacy of our efforts, but also because, in the end, love cannot be earned even by our being perfect. This means that if we are to experience God's love, God must give that love freely, unconditionally, gratuitously: as a "grace." In its simplest terms, this is what we mean when we say we are saved by the grace of God. This is the meaning of the coming of Christ. In Christ the message of God's freely given love for all of humanity is proclaimed. When we respond to this proclamation of God's love with faith (trusting belief), then we no longer live under the law but under grace. Paul, therefore, sees the historical period

beginning with Christ as the period of adulthood in humanity's religious development. It is the time of living "under grace."

The experience of living under the law serves a third purpose of bringing us to an awareness of the true function of the law. If we cannot justify ourselves before God by keeping his law, why did he give us a law in the first place? Paul himself poses this question. If the pattern of salvation is the divine call and promise and the human response of faith, as exemplified by Abraham, why did God introduce the law through Moses hundreds of years later? Paul's answer is that "This was done to specify crimes, until the posterity came to whom the promise was addressed" (Galatians 3:19). Paul sees Christ as the one in whom the promise made to Abraham was fulfilled, since it is in Christ that all the nations of the world are blessed. The time of living under the law, then, seems to be a time of preparation for the coming of Christ and living under grace. Further on Paul says, "The law was to be our guardian until Christ came and we could be justified by faith" (Galatians 3:24). In the life of the individual Christian also, living under the law is a necessary preliminary to living under grace.

Why is this so? I believe that the answer to this question is that our failed attempts to justify ourselves by keeping God's law bring us to an awareness of the true function or purpose of that law. While the law represents the way we should try to live, we must be disabused of the notion that our *attempts* to live up to what the law demands are the means by which we earn God's love. Keeping the moral law is our way of trying to be fully human and fully Christian; it is not a way of earning anything from God. Furthermore, we do not fully appreciate the free gift of God's love unless we have first tried to earn it by our own efforts and failed. Most of us seem to be reluctant to accept "charity." We do so only when our own human resources are exhausted. The honourable poor man must reach a point of being utterly unable to support himself before accepting charity. The adolescent must experience the inadequacy of her idealism before she can receive love and acceptance as a gift and become an adult. And the Christian must experience the inadequacy of moral and religious observance to justify himself before God if he is to be ready to respond with faith to God's freely given love or grace.

## II. The Meaning of Faith

The foundation of the Christian life is the faith by which we believe in and are assured of the gift of God's love. This kind of faith liberates us from the need to constantly prove or justify ourselves and from the self-preoccupation that characterizes such an effort. The assurance of God's gratuitous love is the soil in which we grow to "self-forgetful" Christian adulthood. The "good life" we tried to live in order to prove ourselves worthy and deserving of God's love paradoxically becomes more accessible when it is no longer pursued as a means of self-justification – when it becomes something we *want* to do rather than something we *have* to do. Our human experience seems to confirm this. Imagine that you are called upon to give a speech. You will be much more successful and effective if you have something to say than if you merely have to say something. St. Paul reminds the Christians of Ephesus of this fundamental role of faith in their lives: "It is by grace that you have been saved, through faith; not by anything of your own, but by a gift from God; not by anything you have done, so that nobody can claim the credit. We are God's work of art, created in Christ Jesus to live the good life as from the beginning he had meant us to live it" (Ephesians 2:8-10). The Christian is not a "self-made" man or woman but "God's work of art." Only God's grace makes possible the "good life." Only God's grace – his freely given acceptance of us – relieves us of the necessity of earning that acceptance and makes possible a self-forgetful commitment to moral values for their own sake.

# 6. HOW DOES FAITH CHANGE US?

Chapter 6 of John's gospel tells the story of Jesus' multiplication of the five loaves and the two fish to feed a crowd of 5000 people. The following day, the crowd goes looking for Jesus and, when they find him, he takes the opportunity to remind them that there is a kind of hunger that is deeper than the hunger he satisfied by his miracle of the day before. There is a spiritual hunger for the fullness of life that can only be satisfied by the bread "which comes down from heaven." When the people ask him to give them this bread, Jesus answers: "I am the bread of life. He who comes to me will never be hungry; he who believes in me will never thirst" (John 6:35). Catholic piety rightly associates these words with the sacrament of the Eucharist. The transforming effect of the Eucharist, however, is proportionate to the faith of the recipient. Jesus emphasizes this more fundamental meaning with the words "he who comes to me" and "he who believes in me." The spiritual nourishment implied in the words "bread of life" is for those who come or respond to Jesus with faith. It is faith that brings about the spiritual nourishment and growth of the believer just as material food nourishes us and helps us to grow.

These words of Jesus bring us back to our nagging questions: Why do some people respond to Jesus with faith and others do not? Why do some see Jesus as the "bread of life" while others do not? Some of the Jewish leaders of the time had a difficult time seeing Jesus as the "bread from heaven" with all the spiritual significance that such a phrase implied. After all, was he not merely the son of Joseph the carpenter and his wife, Mary? Like many of us, they were blind to the truth of the Incarnation, that the divine is revealed in the human. Jesus responds to their conundrum with this statement: "No one can come to me unless he is drawn by the Father who sent me" (John 6:44). We have faith because we are somehow "drawn" to Christ by the Father who is revealed in Christ. What does this mean? You will perhaps recall St. Thomas Aquinas' definition of faith (see Chapter 4) in which he asserts that, in the act of faith, the mind's assent is made under the influence of the will, which in turn is "moved by God through grace." This definition by itself does little to resolve the problem of how our act of faith can be an act of human freedom and yet be something we are drawn to by the grace of God. Does God draw us against our will? Is our freedom overruled?

As already noted, Catholic teaching at times left the impression that faith was a "gift" in the sense that God's grace acted as some kind of mysterious agent moving our will to make the act of faith. It was further asserted that this action of God's grace in no way curtailed our human freedom. For most of us, this amounted to a non-explanation since we could not relate it to anything in our human experience. St. Augustine offers what I believe is a better explanation. Commenting on the words of Christ "No one comes to me unless the Father draw him," he offers the following explanation:

> Do not think that you will be drawn against your will; it is love that draws the soul. Fear not that men who juggle words and have not the slightest understanding of divine things may stump us here by asking: "How can I freely believe if I am drawn?" I answer: "You are drawn by your own will indeed, but by delight as well...."
>
> Is the body to have its delights and the soul none?... Give me a lover – he will know what I mean! Give me a man who desires and hungers, a man who wanders in this desert and thirsts for the fountain of the eternal country – he will know what I mean! But if you are unmoved, you do not know what I am talking about.
>
> Show a green branch to a sheep and it will follow you. Show sweets to a child and he will follow you. Persons are drawn by love, by ties of the heart. If delight draws us, will not Christ draw us – he who is the revelation of the Father?[24]

---

[24] *Commentary on John*, Treatise 26.

I am suggesting that this is a better explanation of the role of grace in drawing us to faith for two reasons. First, it is rooted in an understanding of grace not as some mysterious agent – some *thing* that God gives us – but as God's love for us as revealed in Christ. Second, Augustine reconciles the action of grace with our human freedom by relating it to our human experience.

Augustine's explanation is simply this: "Persons are drawn by love, by ties of the heart." When we are drawn to Christ we are drawn by the love of God revealed in his person. Anyone who has had the experience of being in love, Augustine argues, will know what he is talking about. Being in love is a paradoxical experience. People who are in love are subjected to an overpowering attraction over which they have little, if any, control. And yet they do not feel that their freedom has been violated. In fact, they might very well claim that they have never felt freer. In the extravagant language of love, they "surrender," but willingly; they are "prisoners of love" (as the old song puts it), but free and willing prisoners. As Augustine says, we are willingly drawn by what delights us. The "problem" of the conflict between this way of being drawn and our human freedom is a problem created by those who try to solve everything logically, those who "juggle words" in a way that is divorced from human experience. Faith is a free human act, but we are drawn to it by grace because the grace of God is simply the love of God and we are "drawn by love." To have faith is to be moved by God's love for us and to believe in it. If we do not have the capacity to be moved by love – human or divine, we are not likely to have faith – human or divine. As Augustine puts it, "If you are unmoved, you do not know what I am talking about."

When we speak thus – when we speak of being moved by God's love for us – we imply that this love brings about some kind of change or transformation in the believer. If the experience of human love changes people, should we not expect the love of God to have the same kind of transforming power? We often speak of this, but what exactly does it mean? How does our belief in God's love for us change us? Is there a psychological language that would describe a transformation so profound that we describe it as "rebirth" or a "new creation"? Some Christians have so embraced the phrase "born again" that they believe that their old self has in some sense been annihilated and that God's grace has created an entirely new person in its place. To the rest of us, this seems to run contrary to our belief in the essential goodness of what God created in the first place. Consequently, even many Christians who call themselves "born again" would reject this radical view. The alternative is to describe the experience of being "reborn" in terms of self-actualization; rebirth is the at least partial realization of our essential goodness. The love of God (grace) and our response of faith move us in the direction of becoming the persons we were meant to be according to the intent of God's original creation. It does so by effecting a fundamental change of attitude and a radical reorientation of our lives. The religious word for this is "conversion," a change of heart. Insofar as this transformation can be described in human psychological language, I believe it expresses itself in three ways: a new moral attitude, a new kind of motivation and an attitude of self-forgetfulness.

1. *A new moral attitude.* This new moral attitude is what St. Paul refers to as "freedom from the law." We have seen that for those living "under the law," that is, trying to earn God's love by observing the moral law, the purpose of the moral law is, to put it bluntly, to frustrate them. It is only by trying to justify ourselves by such moral efforts and failing that we are led to a point of psychological "readiness" for faith. We are ready to accept the free gift of God's love in faith only when we have proved to ourselves that we cannot earn it, only when our human efforts to deserve it have reached a dead end. For this reason I have suggested that the element of risk in Christian faith involves the giving up of reliance on one's own human goodness. Salvation is not earned; it is a gift. God does not love us because we are good; we are good because God loves us. Faith as the acceptance of God's love and trusting belief in it is only possible when we have given up the illusion of our moral self-sufficiency, our ability to justify ourselves. As St. Paul writes: "What proves that God loves us is that Christ died for us while we were still sinners" (Romans 5:8). Unless we are conscious of being "sinners," we do not fully appreciate that love, nor will our belief in it have the transforming effect of genuine faith. As long as we think that we deserve another person's love, that love will not change us. In the same way, as long as we persist in the illusion that we have earned God's love, we will never experience it as

undeserved love, as grace; nor will we ever be free of the oppressive need to keep earning it.

St. Paul's teaching is that "no one can be justified in the sight of God by keeping the law; all that the law does is tell us what is sinful" (Romans 3:20). The moral law is good in itself because it tells us what is objectively good and evil and holds up to us an ideal of authentically Christian and human living. Nevertheless, it frustrates us because it does not give us the power to live up to that ideal. Our attempts to justify ourselves by observing it lead to guilt, anxiety and frustration. However, in the light of grace – of the reality that God's love is a free gift and not to be earned – we are, in Paul's words, "rid of the law, freed by death from its imprisonment, free to serve in a new spiritual way and not the old way of a written law" (Romans 7:6). The death that has liberated us from the law is the death of Christ. Does this mean that we are free to simply disregard the law and its demands? Paul asks this question: "Does the fact that we are living by grace and not by law mean that we are free to sin?" He answers emphatically: "Of course not!" (Romans 6:15). Clearly we are not liberated from the law in any absolute sense. The law is not to be simply disregarded; it still represents the valid moral principles we want to live by. What we are liberated from is the "oppression" of the law. The law is no longer to be regarded as a means of earning God's love – a project that has become meaningless in the light of grace.

2. *A new kind of motivation.* If the moral law is no longer to be observed with a view to earning God's love and acceptance, what reason does the Christian now have for trying to live a good moral life? If I am reading St. Paul correctly, I understand him to say that being liberated from the need to justify myself before God means not that I am free to disregard the moral law, but that my motive for keeping it is different. It means that we are "free to serve in a new spiritual way." Psychologist Gordon Allport identified the essential dynamic in growing from immaturity to maturity as a "transformation of motives." A young man, for instance, might enter the same profession as his father out of a neurotic, infantile need to identify or compete with his father. In time, however, he comes to see that the profession he is pursuing has a value in itself. Now he finds happiness and fulfillment in the work itself. His ulterior motive

disappears; he has outgrown his childish motivation. His maturity consists not in doing something different but in doing the same work from a different, more mature motive. In the same way, our passage from religious immaturity (living under the law) to religious maturity (living under grace) does not consist in abandoning the pursuit of our moral ideals, but in pursuing them with a different motive. We no longer keep the moral law from an infantile, ulterior need to earn love and approval, but simply because the moral law has been internalized and so represents the way we want to live.

In the light of grace, there is no need for the person of faith to fulfill any conditions in order to earn God's love. There is no need to curry favour or score points with God, no need to be obsessed with myself and my own standing before God. All such motives are self-justifying and consequently self-centred or self-absorbed. I am obeying God and doing good for others, but for a basically self-serving and ulterior motive – to earn God's approval of *me*. Consider the self-preoccupied quality of a religious life obsessed with "saving one's soul." In the light of grace, all such motivation is not only immature but futile. This in turn means that I am free to observe the moral law from a different and more mature motive. Now I can keep the moral law purely and simply because it is the right thing to do; because I believe it is the way a Christian and, for that matter, a human being should live. Such motivation is "self-transcending," that is, free of self-interest and self-concern. The moral life is no longer a way of earning love and approval but a response to a love that has already been given. I now keep the moral law because I want to, not because I have to. By the same token, my moral failures may indeed be occasions for regret and repentance, but they are not seen as causing the loss of God's love, which is independent of any human merit. The love of God is like that of wise parents who make demands and set standards and expectations for their child. It would be ludicrous, however, to think that the child *earns* the parents' love by living up to these expectations.

3. *Self-forgetfulness.* The unconditional love and forgiveness of God that is proclaimed, Christians believe, in the life, death and resurrection of Christ, is a once-and-for-all event. This

means that we always stand under God's love and forgiveness. The life of faith, then, is a life based on and inspired by trusting belief in that love and forgiveness, a life rooted in the confidence and assurance which that love inspires. Scripture is full of passages in which God proclaims his constant fidelity to the covenant he has entered into with his people. The psalmist responds to this fidelity in these words: "O praise the Lord, all you nations, acclaim him all you peoples. Strong is his love for us; he is faithful forever" (Psalm 116). In other words, God is like a faithful marriage partner; his love is constant. Therefore, the faith of the Christian assures her that God's love and forgiveness are always present and are not withdrawn when one is guilty of moral failures. The Christian life is not some kind of continuous cycle of popping in and out of the "state of grace." (Sin…lose God's grace…go to confession…regain God's grace, etc.) In reality, when I confess my moral failures, I do not regain something God has withdrawn. My act of confession is a renewal of my faith in a love and forgiveness that were always there.

The life of faith, then, is a life rooted in the assurance of the constancy of God's freely given love and acceptance. It calls for a new religious attitude that is radically distinct from that of the legalist, who tries to earn that love and acceptance through moral and religious observance. What is there for the asking cannot be earned or deserved. What is perceived as something to be earned cannot be appreciated as a gift. The legalistic attitude has to be given up before an attitude of faith can take root. Otherwise – to borrow Jesus' analogy – it is like trying to patch an old garment with new cloth or like putting new wine into old wineskins (Luke 5:36-39).

This radical change of attitude brings about a change in the believer that is best described by the term "self-forgetfulness." This word has already been used as descriptive of adulthood or maturity. In this context, it simply means that one rises above, outgrows, is liberated from or "transcends" the adolescent kind of self-preoccupation that characterizes life "under the law." If I no longer have to earn God's love (that is, my salvation), I can stop worrying about myself and my standing before God. This question has been answered once and for all. This in turn means that I am free to direct my concern away from myself and towards the welfare, problems and concerns of others. Here, I believe, lies the transforming power of faith. It transforms the believer from a self-preoccupied religious adolescent to a self-forgetful, outer directed religious adult. To be liberated from the necessity of earning God's love and acceptance means to be liberated from the self-absorption that accompanies such an effort. Self-transcendence replaces self-preoccupation. Only when I am liberated from myself and my own petty concerns can I be truly concerned about other people and their problems. In this way, I am enabled to fulfill – admittedly in a partial and fragmentary way – the Christian moral ideal of selfless, altruistic love.

The Christian moral ideal is often misunderstood. Those who strip the person of Jesus of any transcendent significance and depict him as nothing more than a great ethical teacher have missed something very important. Ditto for those who, inspired by Jesus, simply tell us to love one another as if it were the easiest thing in the world. The truth is, if we really take Jesus' ethic of love seriously, it is pretty much impossible to observe by our unaided human efforts. It is not entirely accurate to say that the moral ideal proposed by Jesus was to love our neighbours as we love ourselves. In proposing this ideal, Jesus quotes from the Old Testament in answer to the Jewish scribe who asked him what was the greatest commandment in the Jewish law. Jesus' own moral ideal was enunciated at the Last Supper: "This is my commandment: love one another as I have loved you" (John 15:12). In this ideal of love to the point of death, as well as the examples he gives of this kind of love in action (turning the other cheek, walking the extra mile, etc.), Jesus seems to be going out of his way to emphasize the fact that the moral ideal of love he proposes is beyond human achievement. Ultimately, this is why we cannot earn salvation.

Love, therefore, is not just something we are commanded to practise as Christians. Something so obviously beyond our human capacities cannot be simply commanded. It is something we must, in some way, be rendered capable of achieving. It is through the transforming experience of grace and faith that we are enabled to at least approximate this ideal. We love and are concerned about others to the extent that we are liberated from concern for ourselves by this experience of grace and faith. Self-forgetfulness translates into love for others. That is why Christian tradition makes a connection between faith and the moral life of the Christian. St. Ignatius of Antioch (first century) put it this way: "These are the beginning and goal of life: faith the beginning, love the goal."[25] Genuine faith is meant to increase our capacity for love; it is the beginning of a process whose goal is love. That love, in turn, serves the further goal of creating genuine community.

We should also note that this freedom from self which makes us capable of love is not just a religious goal but a human one as well. Faith, therefore, is not a deterrent to our human development and fulfillment, nor irrelevant to it. It is intended to lead us to the humanly desirable goal of self-transcending adulthood. It is extremely difficult to achieve that goal without being unconditionally loved by one or more other people. Only if we are loved are we capable of loving. The Christian is simply someone who acknowledges this fact and points to God as the ultimate source of such transforming love.

---

[25] *Letter to the Ephesians,* no. 14.

84

# PART III
# THE MORAL LIFE

A legitimate distinction can be made between religion and morality. Christian morality, however, can only be understood in the context of religion. It must be seen first of all as an integral part of the Christian's response of faith to the revelation of God's grace. Second, the Christian moral ideal of self-forgetful, altruistic love is unrealizable apart from the transforming effect of that same experience of grace and faith. In this section, separate chapters are devoted to Christian morality and Catholic morality. This is not to suggest that they are separate entities, but to acknowledge the particular issues dealt with by Catholics, especially those questions raised by the authoritative moral teachings of their Church. This in turn leads us to a more general discussion of the role of the Church in Catholic life. To understand Catholic morality, then, we need to answer these questions:

1) What is the connection between Christian morality and the life of faith?

2) What are the distinctive features of Catholic morality?

3) Do we need the moral guidance of the Church?

# 7. WHAT IS CHRISTIAN MORALITY?

Chapter 6 was an attempt to analyze – as far as that is possible – the transforming effect of the Christian experience of grace and faith. We saw that this experience involved a transformation from living under the law to living under grace and that its effect is threefold. (1) We are "liberated from the law" in the sense that our moral and religious observance is no longer the basis for "earning" our justification before God. God's love is not earned; we *believe* in it because it has been given freely. (2) This in turn means that we are free to keep the moral law from a new motive, not in order to earn something but in response to what has been given freely. For a Christian, the moral question is not so much "What ought I to do?" as "What has been done for me?" Only in the light of this question can we know what we ought to do. The Christian's moral life is a response to what has been received. (3) Finally, the intended effect of living under grace is liberation from the kind of self-preoccupation that characterizes the attempt to earn salvation. To the extent that we are free of self-concern, we are able to be concerned about others and, in a partial and fragmentary way, to fulfill the Christian moral ideal of self-transcending love.

The personal transformation involved in passing from life under the law to life under grace is one way of interpreting the New Testament language that speaks of the "new creation" and the language of "rebirth" associated with baptism. In a sermon on the wedding feast at Cana, fifth-century bishop Faustus of Riez speaks of the changing of water into wine as a symbol of this transformation from law to grace.

> To those who simply see the event at Cana, then, it is a miracle; to those who also understand it, it is a mystery. For in the changed water of Cana we have an image of baptismal rebirth: one substance becomes another; and the lesser, through a hidden change, becomes the greater.

> Through Christ's action in Galilee, water becomes wine; that is, the law passes away and grace takes its place; the shadows pass and truth is revealed.... As the water in the jars does not become something less than it was but begins to be what it had not been, so the law is not destroyed by Christ's coming but is fulfilled. The one wine runs out and another is supplied; the wine of the Old Covenant was good, the wine of the New Covenant is better.[26]

Some interpreters of this story like to downplay the miraculous element and stress the friendliness of Jesus who clearly liked to have a good time with his friends. Others emphasize the miracle as affirming Jesus' divine authority at the beginning of his public life. Bishop Faustus, however, looks beyond even the miracle in order to find the "mystery" it reveals. The mystery is what the miracle symbolizes. The transformation of water into wine symbolizes the transformation that accompanies the transition from law to grace.

Notice, however, that the preacher is careful to point out that the water does not become something less than it was, but becomes something that it was not before. In the same way, he says, the law is not destroyed or rendered insignificant when we begin to live under grace. On the contrary, the law is fulfilled; it realizes its true meaning and destiny. The true function of the law, as we have seen, is not to provide us with a means of justifying ourselves before God. Its true function is to be a preamble to the life of faith; to provide a means of proving to oneself (through failure to observe it) that God's love cannot be earned through one's own human resources. God's love – like anyone else's – is always a gift. Seen in this light, living under the law seems to be a necessary preamble to living under grace. Why is it that many Christians seem content to spend their lives living "under the law," that is, under the illusion that, by their efforts to live a good life, they are earning God's love and making themselves deserving of eternal life? If one were to ask these

---

[26] *Sermons on the Epiphany*, Sermon 5.

same Christians whether their children were behaving well enough to "earn" their love, I am quite sure they would find the question preposterous.

Now, if faith is one's response to God's grace which includes moral commitment, this raises questions: What are the moral consequences of living under grace? What difference does living under grace make for the moral life of the Christian? The most obvious difference is that to live under grace is to experience God's love as an unconditional gift. This in turn means that, since what is given freely cannot be earned, there is nothing to be "earned" by keeping the moral law. When confronted with this truth, one is tempted to conclude that there is no point in "being good," since God will love us in any event. This, however, is a curiously rational approach to what is a human experience and makes sense only within a narrow frame of reference according to which the only reason for "being good" is to earn a reward. A moment's reflection on our human experience should convince us that moral laxity is an unnatural response to unconditional love. Imagine that you have fallen in love and discover to your delight that the object of your affection has also fallen in love with you and loves you in spite of all your human foibles and shortcomings. Would you then use that realization as an excuse to abuse or deceive or ignore your beloved on the grounds that he or she will love you anyway? Is it not more likely that you would consider yourself blessed and make every effort to be worthy of the other's love? Here, in a nutshell, is the essence of Christian morality. It is not an effort to earn love and acceptance but an effort to be worthy of a love that has already been received.

For all this to make sense, however, there is one point in particular that needs to be stressed. In order to respond to another's love by trying to be worthy of it, it must be a love that is valued, a love and acceptance that is deeply needed and desired. In our example from human experience, the love I respond to in this way is the love of someone with whom I am already in love; someone, therefore, whose love I need and value. If a perfect stranger announced his or her unconditional love for me, I would not feel moved to respond in the same manner. Likewise, the message of God's grace elicits this kind of response only if it is a love that is valued, only if it is a love that we are trying to earn. That is why living under the law is a necessary preamble to living under grace. Only those who have tried to earn God's love and failed can respond appropriately when it is offered as a free gift. It is no coincidence that the message of God's grace was first proclaimed to the Jews, a highly religious people and – as the nation chosen to be the recipient of God's law – a people who had gone through the experience of living under the law. It would be an entirely inappropriate response to another's love to continue to insist on trying to earn it. It would be an insult to the other, much like trying to pay for a gift someone has given you. In the same way, when God's grace (love) is offered to us as a gift, it would be wrong to continue to try to earn it or be deserving of it through obser-vance of the moral law. This would amount to a refusal of the gift. In the light of grace, then, sin is not just a matter of failing to keep the moral law. Surely keeping the moral law with the self-righteous intention of rendering oneself *deserving* of God's love is also sinful since it amounts to a refusal of God's grace.

If the moral life of the Christian is a response to God's grace or freely given love, then this gift of love is the foundation of that moral life. It is also the foundation of the moral life in that it liberates us from the self-preoccupation that is the result of living under the law and this freedom from self is intended to empower and liberate us to love others. As Pope Clement I put it, "Who are fitted to be lovers save those whom God makes worthy?"[27] This kind of altruistic, self-forgetful love, then, becomes both the measure of the depth of our faith and the ultimate criterion and ideal against which we measure the moral quality of our lives. This is not surprising since by faith we enter into a *personal* relationship with God, and love is the ultimate measure of anyone's fidelity and commitment to a personal relationship – such as between friends, lovers, spouses, or parents and children. Abraham responded to God's summons with faith and thereby entered into a "covenant" with God, which took the form of a formal contract (Genesis 15). The Christian enters by faith into a "new covenant" with God that takes the form of a personal relationship in which God becomes our father and we his children. As the text of the Mass reminds

---

[27] *Letter to the Corinthians,* 50:2.

us, Jesus "taught us" to call God our Father. And St. Paul writes: "Everyone moved by the Spirit is a son of God. The spirit you received is not the spirit of slaves bringing fear into your lives again; it is the spirit of sons, and it makes us cry out, 'Abba, Father!' The Spirit himself and our spirit bear united witness that we are children of God" (Romans 8:14-16).

Notice that Paul attributes our status as children of God to the fact that we have received the Holy Spirit. The gift of the Spirit, then, is the principle of the Christian's personal relationship with God. In order to understand this, it should be remembered that we are talking about the Holy Spirit, the third person of the Trinity. At the risk of grossly oversimplifying, let us think of the Trinity as follows: the Father exists from eternity as a being capable of knowledge and love (since these are the marks of personhood). But apart from and "before" his creation, what does he know and love? The answer can only be "himself." His knowledge of himself – what we might call his self-image – is an idea that so perfectly reflects or expresses the person of the father that it is another person – the Son or the Word – who is the exact image of the Father. It is as if I looked into a mirror and the reflected image was so perfect that it was "another me." Now between the Father and the Son there is a bond of love. *The Holy Spirit is the bond of love between the Father and the Son.* To receive the Holy Spirit, therefore, is to participate in that bond of love between Father and Son; to be taken up into and given a share in the relationship of the Son to the Father; to relate to God as to a father, as the Son does. This relationship is a personal relationship that goes beyond a mere relationship of law. All obedience to moral law should be seen as an attempt to be faithful to this personal relationship. Not only does the gift of the Spirit create an ideal of love in personal relatedness; it empowers the Christian to love in return, since the Spirit, as the bond between Father and Son, represents the love of God. Hence, St. Paul writes: "The love of God has been poured into our hearts by the Holy Spirit which has been given us" (Romans 5:5). In Chapter 6 we tried to understand this gift of the capacity or ability to love in the human terms of the power of another person's gift of love to liberate us from self-preoccupation so that our love and concern may be directed towards others.

## III. The Moral Life

If the experience of grace and faith initiates a personal relationship with God, then that relationship is no longer a legal one in which one must live up to the demands of the law in order to render oneself acceptable to God. This does not mean that the moral law is simply ignored but that a new attitude towards the law and a new motive for keeping it become possible. (See Chapter 6.) At the heart of this new attitude is a set of convictions about this new relationship with God – a relationship to be viewed in the light of grace. First is the conviction that our justification before God is through grace (God's freely given love) and faith (one's belief in that love), not something to be earned through observance of law. We are the objects of God's love because he bestows that love freely, not because we are deserving of it. Second, in the light of grace, we realize that our justifying relationship with God is not the *result* of our moral efforts but the *cause* of those efforts. In other words, God's unconditional love and acceptance does not come about as a reward for our efforts to live morally. Rather, we strive to live morally in response to that love and acceptance. The moral life is a response to God's love, not an effort to earn that love. This, I believe, is what St. Paul meant when he spoke of being "liberated from the law." It does not mean that the moral law no longer has any force or function in the life of the Christian. It does mean that the moral law is no longer something oppressive and threatening. It represents an ideal to shoot for, not a requirement for earning salvation. To be liberated from the law, then, means to be relieved of the necessity of earning one's salvation through observance of the law.

But if the Christian has been liberated from the necessity of earning salvation, what motive is left for keeping the moral law? Here are some suggestions from a couple of first-century experts.

St. Paul tells us that by our baptism we are incorporated into Christ and participate in his death and resurrection; we "die" to sin and "rise" to a new life. Sin is, therefore, antithetical to the new life in Christ. "You have been taught that when we were baptized in Christ Jesus we were baptized in his death; in other words, when we were baptized we went into the tomb with him and joined him in death, so that as Christ was raised from the dead by the Father's glory, we too might live a new life" (Romans 6:3-4). Moreover, he points out that sin is a form of slavery that is incompatible with one's status as a Christian (Romans 6:15-19). It might be helpful to recall that Paul describes his experience of living under the law with its experience of sin and guilt as a kind of "death." Perhaps the death the Christian must experience in order to live in Christ and in his grace is the death-like experience of sin and guilt. Even from the point of view of human growth and human values, hateful, malicious, envious and deceitful attitudes can be seen as enslaving and death-like in the sense that they stunt our human and spiritual growth. Paul reminds Christians that the grace of God is meant to liberate them from that kind of slavery and death. They are free to live a new kind of life and the moral law is a guide for living that new life.

Pope Clement I speaks in a similar vein. Having stated the principle that we are justified "not by our own efforts – our wisdom or understanding or piety or good deeds – but by faith," he then asks: "What conclusion shall we draw from all this? To cease our good works and to neglect love?" And he answers:

> Not at all! Rather we must hasten to every good work with joyful diligence, since the Maker and Lord of all rejoices in all that he has made. When he had finished everything else, he shaped with his own hands the most excellent creature of all, man, and stamped him with his own image. Therefore the just have always been intent upon good works.[28]

We pursue a morally good life, he maintains, because in this way we reflect the image of God in which we were created. The "just" – those who are "justified," who therefore already are assured of God's love and acceptance and have no need to earn

---

[28] *Letter to the Corinthians,* 33:1-7

it – are nevertheless "intent upon good works." Why? Because in this way they are being true to their identity as children of God, created in God's image. It is a matter of integrity, of acting according to what you are. The reasons given by both Paul and Clement for keeping the moral law have nothing to do with earning or making oneself deserving of anything from God.

The third conviction at the heart of this new attitude to the moral law is the conviction that the observance of the moral law does not fully express or exhaust the meaning of this new relationship with God that is rooted in faith. This is not a legal relationship but a *personal* one. A legal relationship – one that is defined by a written law – is essentially static. My obligations in a legal relationship (e.g., under criminal or civil law or according to the terms of a legal contract) do not change unless the law is amended or the terms of the contract renegotiated. The law imposes on an individual a set of obligations that define what is to be done, no more and no less. Tax laws determine the exact amount of taxes I must pay. Traffic laws tell me exactly what the speed limit is. Criminal law establishes exactly what constitutes an offence and distinguishes between varying degrees of responsibility. A personal relationship is not like this; its demands cannot be codified. My obligations to my spouse, children, etc., are not static; they require sensitivity to changing needs and circumstances. Parents cannot treat their 16-year-old as they did when he or she was six. Consider the case of the average family and its network of responsibilities. In most families there is an understanding regarding who does what: who does the cooking or laundry, who takes the kids to hockey practice, and even – if they are masters of compromise – who controls the TV remote! As children mature they, too, are given household responsibilities. If one had a mind to, these responsibilities could be codified in a written list and posted on the refrigerator door. Would it not be ludicrous, however, to think that these "rules" express the essential meaning of that family or that their faithful observance of them is what keeps the family together?

What is it, then, that holds spouses, lovers, friends, parents and children together? What is the principle of such relationships if it is not law or rules? The answer, of course, is love. Love is the "spirit" that cements personal relationships. In this respect, there is an analogy between human personal relationships and the faith relationship between God and the Christian believer. In both cases what defines the relationship is not a set of laws or rules but a certain "spirit." St. Paul identifies the principle of our relationship with God as the Holy Spirit who has been given to us. In the same way, a human relationship is held together by a certain "spirit" – a set of shared feelings, attitudes, memories, etc. It is this spirit that ultimately holds people together and dictates their conduct towards each other. We all understand this, but often fail to apply this understanding to our relationship with God, to the Holy Spirit who is the source of that relationship and to the moral obligations inherent in that relationship. If our faith relationship with God is a truly personal one, why is it that we can just as easily interpret its moral obligations in purely moralistic, legalistic terms, as if God were not a father but a lawgiver? If our relationship with God is truly personal, it is not static and governed by the static demands of law; it is, like any other personal relationship, organic, open-ended and subject to growth. This means that ultimately its demands cannot be fixed in a static code. There is a limit to what law obliges me to do; there is no limit to what I want to do for someone I love. Nor can any set of rules tell me exactly what needs to be done for that loved one in every circumstance. The demands of a personal relationship go beyond concrete rules, beyond what St. Paul called the "letter of the law."

When we say that a personal relationship is open-ended and subject to change, we thereby imply that carrying out one's responsibilities within that relationship involves sensitivity to changing circumstances and the changing needs of the loved one. The love of a parent for a child is a case in point. Sometimes the child needs control, sometimes freedom; sometimes cheering up or encouragement, sometimes a stern "talking to"; sometimes a show of affection, sometimes discipline. But all are expressions of love and concern – a love and concern that cannot be codified in a set of concrete rules. ("Be flexible" is not a very concrete rule.) Without such concrete rules to fall back on, the certainty of being always "in the right" is impossible to achieve, as every parent knows. In the case of one's relationship with God, it is not God's needs and circumstances that change but our own and those of the world around us. As in any personal relationship, however, there is a moral standard that goes beyond the letter of the law or concrete rules. The moral law, of course, remains the guideline and framework for responding to the revelation of God's grace. But the ultimate moral standard is something beyond law. The ultimate moral obligation is to the demands of one's personal relationship with God. That is why sin is ultimately not the breaking of a law, but the failure to love: the failure to respond to the demands of one's personal faith relationship with God. Love is the essence of fidelity to that relationship. Hence St. Augustine's famous statement "Love and do what you will." Jesus himself reminds us that when we have done everything required of us by duty (by law) we can still regard ourselves as "unprofitable servants" (Luke 17:10).

These two statements may be combined as follows: if we truly love, we have kept the law because what we want to do will correspond with what we ought to do. On the other hand, it is possible to keep the letter of the law dutifully but without love and, therefore, in a way that is ultimately unprofitable. Marc Oraison sums up this morality of personal relationship in this way: "All *sin*, whatever it is, is a refusal of the Other, a flaw in the texture of love, a closing in upon oneself. If it is not conceived as such, it is no longer 'sin' but an infraction of the 'law' and this attitude is no longer really religious or Christian."[29] If we understand that Christian morality is a morality of fidelity to a personal relationship (or covenant), then we understand that it is a morality of love rather than law. I believe that it is important to understand this aspect of Christian morality for the following four reasons:

1. *It makes for peace of mind.* "Peace be with you," Christ said to his apostles, and we wish that same peace to each other at every Mass. There is little peace to be found in the anxiety-ridden and self-absorbed effort to earn God's love through moral effort, in living "under the law." To live under grace, however, is to live with the assurance of God's unconditional

---

[29] *Love or Constraint?* (New York: P.J. Kenedy and Sons, 1959), p. 125.

love in spite of the limited success of one's moral striving. If the moral life is a response to God's love within the context of a personal relationship, one is free to aim at a higher ideal than the letter of the law, knowing that failure to be perfect will not mean the loss of the Other's love. Is this not also the case in our human personal relationships? Those relationships are not threatened by the fact that we are not perfect. When we try to respond to someone who already loves us, we do not suffer the anxiety of trying to earn that love. Our flawed efforts to return that love are not fraught with anxiety, since we know that we are not loved for being perfect. Such freedom from anxiety means peace of mind. The great Protestant theologian Karl Barth points out that the effect of grace is a new, relaxed attitude to oneself and one's achievements in which anxiety is replaced by a feeling of security. "I can regard myself," he writes, "as secure in my heart. I can think my few thoughts in peace, say my few words in peace, do my few works in peace."[30] The legalist, who believes that God's love must be earned by scrupulous observance of God's law, will never know that kind of peace. This person cannot afford to be imperfect.

2. *It helps us to understand the meaning of freedom of conscience.* The *Catechism of the Catholic Church* (#1790) tells us that "a human being must always obey the certain judgment of his conscience." In Chapter 8 the question of reconciling this freedom of conscience with the Church's moral teachings will be discussed at greater length. For the moment, it should be noted that no one who could be considered a moral person enjoys *absolute* freedom of conscience. To be a moral agent implies that one makes moral decisions within a framework of convictions about what is objectively right or wrong. Even if these moral principles are those taught by the Church, I must internalize them and make them my own if they are truly to be moral guidelines for me. Freedom of conscience, then, is not absolute; it is not simply the freedom to do as one pleases. It is the freedom to act according to one's personal and deeply held moral convictions and principles. It also includes the freedom to act contrary to accepted moral principles out of obedience to a higher law. For the Christian, that higher law is the law of one's

---

[30] *Church Dogmatics,* IV, 1 (Edinburgh: T&T Clark, 1957), p. 774.

personal faith relationship with God. The demands of that relationship take precedence over and relativize the ordinary moral law to which one is committed. Ultimately, the Christian's moral commitment is to his or her relationship to God, or to what we have traditionally called the "will of God." What the Christian ought to do is the will of God; the moral law is a guideline to help us discover what the will of God is.

3. *It demonstrates the limits of the "situation" in helping us to make moral decisions.* The proponents of "situation ethics" (see Chapter 8) tell us that the fundamental Christian imperative – "to do the most loving thing" – is relative to the "situation." This means that every moral decision is a response to the demands of a particular situation or set of circumstances; one must decide what is right (the most loving thing to do), not in a general or abstract way but for that situation. It is the situation, then, that determines one's moral decision. The circumstances themselves, it is claimed, give us moral insight as to what is the most loving thing to do. It is by studying the situation that we determine whether it is morally right and good to steal, lie, have an abortion or drop a nuclear bomb in that situation. While it is true that circumstances must be taken into account in any moral decision-making, New Testament scholar Robin Scroggs reminds us that there is an even more important factor. "More depends," he argues, "upon the quality of the existence of the ethical agent than upon the situation itself. The situation will never tell us the right thing to do, as long as we are blinded by the project of securing our own existence and are therefore impotent to act for the other."[31]

The "project of securing our own existence" refers to the self-absorbed attempt to justify oneself by observance of the moral law. In other words, I will never truly know what is best for someone else as long as I am preoccupied with myself. Freedom from self-preoccupation, the freedom to love others that results from the experience of grace and faith, is the basis for true moral insight. Studying the situation does not tell us what is the right thing to do unless we already love others. St. Paul seems to make the same point: "My prayer is that your love for each other may increase more and more and never stop

---

[31] *Paul for a New Day* (Philadelphia: Fortress Press, 1977), p. 71.

improving your knowledge and deepening your perception so that you can always recognize what is best" (Philippians 1:9-10). Notice Paul's emphasis. It is not rationally deduced moral insight that leads to loving moral action; it is love for others that leads to moral insight (recognizing "what is best").

4. *It identifies what is distinctive about Christian morality*. It is frequently pointed out that when it comes to morally good behaviour, Christians are not significantly better than others. There is no way of knowing whether this is true in some statistical sense. Nevertheless, it seems to be confirmed by our casual observations and by the fact that some of our world's worst scoundrels are at least nominally Christian. It would be a mistake, however, to think that the purpose of the Christian message is to produce a morally superior community. The Christian community is, in the first instance, a community of "sinners," of people who know that they always stand in need of God's forgiving grace. It is that same grace that provides a key to understanding the distinctive character of Christian morality. The Christian moral life is a response to the grace or love of God. Moreover, the Christian moral ideal can only be fulfilled (and then only in a partial way) through the transforming power of that grace. What is distinctive, then, about the Christian moral life is its self-transcending motivation and the source of that motivating power. It does not propose an ethical ideal that can be fulfilled through human willpower. The Christian must be rendered capable of the ideal of love through the liberating experience of grace and faith.

This means that the Christian moral life is inseparably linked to religion; the practice of altruistic, self-forgetful love is dependent on the transforming effect of grace. This is what takes it beyond the realm of that ordinary moral development that is an aspect of our overall human development. The question of the development of moral reasoning, the reasons we give for our moral decisions, has become a question of great interest to developmental psychologists in our own times. This interest is largely due to the work of Lawrence Kohlberg (1927–1987) of Harvard University. Kohlberg's research led him to propose that human moral decision-making develops in six stages. These stages describe the kind of reasoning that motivates our moral behaviour over the course of our human development – from fear of punishment (Stage 1) to adherence to what are held to be universally valid moral principles such as the golden rule (Stage 6). Kohlberg himself, however, realized that these stages were based only on principles of justice and did not explain the kind of altruistic, self-sacrificing love he observed in people like Mother Teresa or Martin Luther King. This led him to speculate about the possibility of a "Stage 7" of moral development. He concluded that the moral motivation of Stage 7 would require some kind of transforming religious or mystical experience. For the Christian believer, this is the experience of grace and faith. What is distinctive about Christian morality is that it proposes a moral ideal that is beyond human achievement and requires the transforming power of grace to fulfill.

Those who try to *earn* their salvation by watering down this Christian ideal of love and turn it into an observable law are pursuing an impossible goal of self-justification. Those who insist that it is sufficient to "love" others without necessarily "liking" them do so for the sake of the false security that comes from being in the right or keeping the law. On the other hand, those who take Christ's ideal of love seriously must live with the constant awareness of falling short of the mark. They live not with the "security" of having kept the law, but with the confidence that God accepts them in spite of their flawed efforts. The "way" that Christ proclaims involves aiming high even in the face of frequent failures. In the midst of one's flawed attempts to follow this way, St. Thomas Aquinas offers this good advice: "It is better to limp along the true way than to walk fearlessly apart from it."[32]

It is better to pursue the true ideal of Christian love, even if the awareness of one's inadequacy makes one "limp," than to stride confidently towards a distorted and falsified version of that ideal. Like the sick, who are aware of their need for the doctor, true Christians are aware that even their best efforts stand in need of forgiveness. In this sense they are the "sinners" whom Christ calls ahead of the self-styled "virtuous" (Matthew 9:12-13).

---

[32] *Commentary on John,* chap. 14.

# 8. WHAT IS CATHOLIC MORALITY?

Thirty years ago the English translation of Father Marc Oraison's book *Morality for Our Time* was published. As both priest and psychologist, Oraison delivered a scathing critique of the moralism and legalism into which Catholic moral teaching had fallen. To illustrate the point, he quotes from a French manual of moral theology of the day entitled *Théologie Morale Catholique* [Catholic Moral Theology]. The opening paragraph of this text describes "morality in general" as follows:

> Man must attain his last end by his personal activity in conformity with the remote (objective) rule and the proximate (subjective) rule of moral action, namely, law and conscience respectively. These rules are violated by sin; their observance is facilitated by the virtues. From this the division of morality in general stems.[33]

Note that in this work of moral "theology," morality is defined without any reference to the theological realities we have been discussing – the grace of God and our human response of faith, which includes moral commitment. According to this manual, morality is divorced from the experience of grace and faith. Moral decision-making is seen to have only two points of reference: abstract law and our subjective conscience. One's relationship with God and others does not seem to enter the picture. It is difficult to see anything theological about a moral theology that relates me only to an abstract law and to myself. As Oraison remarks, the Christian "knows perfectly well that man will attain his last end by the grace of God, and yet, as far as the manual is concerned, nothing could be less to the point."[34]

---

[33] *Morality for Our Time,* trans. by Nels Challe (Garden City, NY: Doubleday, 1969), p. 46.

[34] *Morality for Our Time,* p. 46.

When moral teachings are separated from faith in this way, then moral "theology" ceases to be theology at all. It becomes a series of legalistic, hairsplitting rules about what is "forbidden" and what is "permitted" – rules that are far removed from the real problems of life. Again, Oraison quotes from the manual in question:

> To kill oneself indirectly is *forbidden* in itself, but it can be *permitted* for a proportionally grave reason. This is why it is permitted to work in foundries, mines, glassworks, chemical factories, etc. In the case of cancer, blood poisoning, etc., amputation of a limb is *permitted*. Conjugal relations are *permitted* when they are carried out in view of the procreation of children or for another honest reason.[35]

Notice the obsession with covering every possible situation with rules about what is permitted or forbidden; surely this is the kind of moral guidance one gives to a child. Notice also how unrelated to reality the rules are. It is difficult to imagine an unemployed worker agonizing over whether he has a "proportionally grave reason" for accepting a job in a mine or chemical factory. As for having an "honest reason" for "conjugal relations," I'm sure the average couple would find the question puzzling. In the real world, the moral questions would have to do with the morality of dangerous working conditions and the quality of the total marriage relationship.

The ultimate problem with this kind of morality is that it relates us to a set of abstract rules. If we reject it, it is because we know that true morality relates us in a dynamic way to other persons; Christian morality is also meant to relate us to God who is a living person. If this kind of legalistic morality relates us to God at all, it is not to the God who has proclaimed his love for us in Christ and has promised us the fullness of life, but to a God who is, in Oraison's words, "a menacing policeman of sorts

---

[35] *Morality for Our Time*, p. 52. (Italics mine)

whose role and intention is to assure compliance with the law."[36] The richness and wisdom of Catholic moral teaching will never be appreciated if it is confused with this kind of arid legalism. The question to ponder is this: Have Catholics in general outgrown this legalistic understanding of God and morality? There is no doubt that since Vatican II many Catholics have developed a more mature approach to moral decision-making, at least to the point of realizing that moral conduct cannot be measured simply with reference to abstract rules and prohibitions. Particularly in matters of sexual morality, habits of obedience to the Church's moral teachings have given way to a tendency to question those teachings and to follow one's own conscience.

I am not entirely certain, however, that the growing autonomy of conscience among Catholics since Vatican II represents, in all cases, a sign of mature Christian conscience. More than 30 years after the Council, the tendency to think of morality strictly in terms of obedience to Church teachings seems to be alive and well. This tendency seems to be rooted in a lack of clarity about the relative roles of conscience and Church teaching in making moral decisions. Although it seems to be a dead issue for most Catholics today, the Church's teaching on birth control is a case in point. The very fact that it is a dead issue – a widely ignored teaching – perhaps makes it a useful example of the kind of confusion we are talking about. At the end of the Second Vatican Council, Pope Paul VI established a special commission to study the question of birth control. This commission eventually submitted a report recommending a change in the Church's stand on contraception. After much agonizing, Pope Paul – apparently won over by Vatican conservatives – issued the encyclical letter *Humanae Vitae* [On Human Life], in which he rejected the recommendations of the special commission and reaffirmed what journalists like to call the traditional "ban" on artificial means of birth control. The encyclical was greeted with shock and dismay by large numbers of both laity and clergy. Sociologist and priest Andrew Greeley reports that, immediately after Pope Paul's birth control encyclical, weekly church attendance by U.S. Catholics dropped

---

[36] *Morality for Our Time*, p. 49.

from 70 percent to 50 percent. This episode raises at least two questions.

1. *Was the Pope's teaching on birth control "wrong"?* This begs a further question: What exactly did Pope Paul teach in *Humanae Vitae*? To answer this question fully, one would have to read the entire encyclical. Most people, however, without actually reading the encyclical, simply received it as a statement forbidding artificial means of contraception. There is more to the document, however, than a mere statement of prohibition. It is also a statement of the ideals that should inform and guide a Christian marriage. It reminds us that marriage calls for generosity of body and spirit and self-sacrificing love. Married love, we are told, must be fully human, total, faithful and creative. It is to be a "loving interchange" that brings new life into being (#9). The vast majority of Catholics would agree with this. Then there is an almost audible shifting of gears as a discussion of *ideals and aspirations* is reduced to a *rule* prohibiting artificial means of birth control. After stating the principle that responsible parenthood must be practised with reference to the objective moral order established by God *of which a right conscience is the true interpreter,* Pope Paul then arrives at the curious conclusion that, in the service of transmitting life, married couples are not free to act as they choose or decide for themselves what is the right course to follow (#10). Perhaps the pope was referring to those who choose without any reference to an objective moral order, but the average Catholic could be excused for finding a contradiction here. Does individual conscience have the right to interpret the demands of the divine moral order in this instance or not? Especially given that this statement is followed by a prohibition: "Any use whatever of marriage must retain its natural potential to procreate human life" (#11). It was this concrete prohibition that got everyone's attention and blinded us to the deeper values discussed in the rest of the encyclical. Here, I believe, is a good example of St. Paul's distinction between the "spirit" of the law and the "letter" of the law. If the focus is exclusively on the letter of the law, on the legal prescription or prohibition (in this case, against artificial contraception), the spirit of the law, the values and ideals that the letter is supposed to promote, gets lost. According to St. Paul, it is the spirit that "gives life," while the letter "kills."

If there is anything "wrong" with this encyclical it lies, I would suggest, in this confusion between spirit and letter, which tends to create a false conscience. We know very well that, even at the time of this encyclical, there were many Catholic couples who, for one reason or another, were using artificial means of birth control but, as spouses and parents, were sincerely trying to live up to the ideals of generosity and self-sacrificing love called for by the encyclical. Many of these couples thought the encyclical branded them as "sinners." Defenders of the pope's teaching argued that contraception was "intrinsically evil" in that it interferes with a natural procreative process. This is presented as a conclusion of Catholic "natural law morality," but it is surely not natural law morality at its best. The average Catholic – untutored in the intricacies of moral theology – will immediately detect a flaw in this reasoning. Surely it is wrong to reduce human sexuality to a biological process, and surely it is wrong to make that biological process and not the total well-being of the human and family relationship the ultimate criterion of morality in this case.

2. *How should Catholics have responded to the Church's teaching on birth control?* More than 30 years after Pope Paul's encyclical, we have reached a point where the Church's teaching on birth control is widely ignored by Catholics. In view of this, our question seems moot. And yet I wonder if simply ignoring the teaching – even out of some deep intuitive conviction – is ultimately satisfying to an adult conscience. Moral seriousness demands that we make the right moral decisions but also that we understand *why* we make those decisions. The immediate reaction to Pope Paul's encyclical in 1968 was varied. Some Catholics tried to obey the Pope's directive whatever the difficulties. Others reacted with anger. There were scenes of Catholics walking out of church as their parish priest tried to explain the encyclical to them. Many of these left the Church, never to return. In both of these groups, people were undoubtedly following their consciences in all sincerity. And yet it seems to me that their consciences were badly formed. Both groups looked for a change in the Church's teaching so that they could practise contraception *with the Church's permission*! Is this not the crux of the problem? Moral decision-making based on what is permitted or forbidden by an external authority (pa-

rents, Church, state, etc.) is surely the moral attitude of a child who thinks only in terms of what is "allowed." In this case, the external authority is the Church. Some blindly obeyed the Church's prohibition, thus avoiding any personal input or painful decision-making. The decision was made for them and that was the end of the matter. The second group rebelled, but their rebellion did not necessarily demonstrate a more mature or autonomous conscience. They refused to obey and left the Church, assuming that unquestioning obedience was a condition of membership. The basic premise of their moral decision-making differed little from that of the first group.

Unquestioning obedience is not the proper response for any Catholic to the Church's moral teachings, however. There are two reasons for this. First, mature decision-making requires us to assume personal responsibility for our moral decisions. We cannot abdicate personal responsibility or hand it over to any authority, including the Church. Second, that same Church teaches us that we must follow the dictates of our conscience. This principle is unequivocally stated in the *Catechism of the Catholic Church* (#1790). That is why the reaction of a third group to the 1968 encyclical is instructive. I am referring to those who saw no real conflict between their use of contraception – as an economic, physical or emotional necessity – and the moral teaching of the Church. They also saw that there was no necessary conflict between their use of contraception and a generous, self-sacrificing commitment to their marriage. Why did they see no conflict? Because they realized that even something the Church deems to be an intrinsic moral evil might be *the lesser of two evils* in a given set of circumstances. Life does not always give us a choice between absolute good and absolute evil; often the only choice is between two courses of action, both of which are evil. Our only option is to choose, as best we can, the lesser of the two evils. The police sharpshooter who kills a hostage-taker or the soldier who kills in defence of his country have both done something "intrinsically evil" (killing). Under the circumstances, however, what they did was deemed the lesser of two evils. Therefore, we normally do not hold them morally guilty or culpable. In other words, it is an evil but not a sin. What is intrinsically evil *in principle* may be permissible or morally justifiable in certain circumstances. *It is the moral agent –*

*the person in the circumstances – who must assume responsibility for making this decision.* It is also Catholic teaching, of course, that one should not do something evil to bring about something good. All one can say is that choices about birth control, or even abortion, are clearly *experienced* by the average person as choices between two evils. Most people who have to make such a choice would feel that they are not choosing evil to bring about good; they are choosing one evil to avoid a greater evil. To borrow William James' distinction, it is a "forced" decision – a situation in which one of the options must be chosen. This is not the same as an "avoidable" decision. A government, for instance, that pursued a program of genetic engineering in which a large portion of the population was sterilized against its will in order to create a superior race would clearly be choosing an entirely avoidable evil in order to bring about something it believed to be good.

To many Catholics, the application of this principle to the question of birth control may seem quite unnecessary since, quite frankly, they have a difficult time seeing contraception as something "intrinsically evil." By way of clarification, therefore, let us look at a much more contentious issue: abortion. Here again the Church's moral teaching is clear: Abortion – the termination of a human life – is killing and, therefore, is an intrinsic moral evil. Among Catholics there is much less opposition to this teaching "in principle." Even those who consider themselves "pro-choice" do not consider abortion as something good in itself. The question then becomes this: Under what conditions, if any, would an abortion be morally permissible? Most pro-choice advocates give the pregnant woman an unrestricted right to make this choice. At the other end of the spectrum, many pro-life advocates seem to believe that there are no justifying grounds for an abortion. Most Catholics would agree that, objectively speaking, abortion is a moral evil. If we apply the principle stated above, then the question becomes this: Are there circumstances in which an abortion would be the lesser of two evils and, therefore, morally permissible? If so, then it becomes a decision of individual conscience. Some militant anti-abortionists do not seem to allow for such an exercise of individual conscience. In their minds there are no mitigating circumstances; abortion is "always a sin" and they seem confident that this is the exact position of the Church. I find this attitude disturbing for the following two reasons:

1. *It denies the principle of the "lesser of two evils"* that the Church has historically applied to all forms of killing. On the issue of abortion, one should be willing to at least entertain this question: If something that is intrinsically evil is permissible when circumstances make it the lesser of two evils, should this principle not apply also to the intrinsic evil of abortion? For anyone who has strong convictions about the evil of abortion, there is hesitation in answering this question since, unlike the question of birth control, it is difficult to imagine a set of circumstances that might render an abortion the lesser of two evils. This difficulty is compounded by the fact that, in this case of killing, the victim is innocent.

Having said this, I invite the reader to consider the following case. The famous Viennese psychotherapist, Dr. Viktor Frankl, and his fiancée were married shortly after the Nazi occupation of Austria. In due time Mrs. Frankl became pregnant. During her pregnancy, the Nazi government decreed that all pregnant Jewish women were to be sent immediately to a prison camp. It was well known that this meant certain death for both mother and child. To avoid this, the Frankls decided that she should have an abortion. This left them with the hope that, if they survived their own eventual imprisonment, they would be able to have a family. Since Mrs. Frankl did not survive the prison camp, this hope was not realized. Nevertheless, can anyone seriously question the morality of their decision, which had to weigh this hope against the certainty of death for Mrs. Frankl and her unborn child? How many of us would have done otherwise? Almost 30 years after this abortion, Viktor Frankl dedicated his book *The Unheard Cry for Meaning* "to Harry or Marion, an unborn child." The fact that, after so many years, Frankl was still grieving for his unborn child indicates that this moral decision was not made lightly.

But does that make the Frankls' decision a correct one? It may well be – the situation of the Frankls notwithstanding – that there are no circumstances that would make an abortion the lesser of two evils. What I am suggesting is that to say that abortion is "always a sin" is just as much a fallacy as maintaining that it is justified under certain predetermined conditions (rape, severe health problems, etc.). In both instances the morality of the act is being prejudged and nothing is left to individual conscience. Moreover, to judge every abortion as a "sin" is to judge the one who has the abortion as a "sinner" – something of which the Saviour took a dim view. If Mrs. Frankl had decided against having an abortion, we might well admire her heroic virtue. But heroic virtue cannot be *demanded* of anyone – except, of course, by those moralists who ponder such questions only in the abstract.

2. *It does not reflect the moral teaching of the Church.* The Church does not teach that abortion is "always a sin." It does teach that abortion is a "grave moral evil." This is the kind of phrase used by Pope John Paul II in his encyclical *Evangelium Vitae* [The Gospel of Life], which deals with "life issues" such as birth control, euthanasia, abortion and capital punishment. This *objective* moral principle must be applied to concrete circumstances by the conscience of the individual. Even though mitigating circumstances might be rare, we must still insist, in principle, that what is objectively evil might, in a certain set of circumstances, be the lesser of two evils. Pope John Paul recognizes the fact that one's personal circumstances influence the degree of subjective guilt of those who decide to do something that is, objectively speaking, morally evil:

> Decisions that go against life sometimes arise from difficult or even tragic situations of profound suffering, loneliness, a total lack of economic prospects, depression and anxiety about the future. *Such circumstances can mitigate even to a notable degree subjective responsibility and the consequent culpability of those who make these choices which in themselves are evil.*[37]

If the pope recognizes the mitigating effect of personal circumstances (as the Church has always done), surely those who insist that abortion or anything else is "always a sin" are

---

[37] *Evangelium Vitæ,* #18.

being "more Catholic than the pope." Even what is objectively evil is not always a sin. Under what circumstances would it be the lesser of two evils? The informed individual conscience must make this sometimes terrible decision with full awareness that it might be the wrong decision. In this respect, it is like most of the important decisions one makes in life: it can only be made in good faith, not with absolute certainty of being right. Difficult moral decisions cannot be made with absolute certainty. They can only be made in good faith which, for the Christian, means according to what one sincerely believes is consistent with fidelity to one's faith relationship with God. This distinction between "moral evil" and "sin" should help us understand three important facts about Catholic morality.

1. *Catholic moral teaching is more about values than about rules.* To stay with our example of abortion, the "pro-life" theme that runs through the whole of Catholic moral teaching cannot be reduced to simply a "prohibition" of abortion. "Pro-life" does not simply mean "anti-abortion." The whole gamut of Catholic morality is solidly pro-life in the sense that it is rooted, as Pope John Paul reminds us, in the Christian revelation that reveals to humanity "not only the boundless love of God who 'so loved the world that he gave his only Son' (John 3:16), but also *the incomparable value of every human person.*"[38] To be "pro-life" does not mean merely to condemn abortion; it means to uphold the value of every human life and the dignity of every human person. A committed Catholic is not merely one who obeys rules, but one who tries to live by a set of values that are derived from the mystery of God's self-revelation in Christ. A mature moral agent does not simply obey concrete rules but tries to actualize moral values in the concrete circumstances of his or her life.

2. *Catholic moral teachings presuppose a commitment to these values.* They are directed at those who have committed themselves to living a Christian life; they are guidelines for those who have made such a commitment. If such a commitment is lacking, they may appear to be arbitrary impositions. Sometimes the Church performs this teaching task well, at other times, not so well. But what kind of a Church would it be if it did not even attempt to carry out the task?

---

[38] *Evangelium Vitæ*, #2. (Italics mine)

3. *Though circumstances may be a factor in determining what is a "sin," they do not determine what is "morally evil."* This is one point of differentiation between Catholic morality and "situation ethics." The situationist believes that circumstances can make abortion or killing or dropping a nuclear bomb not just excusable but good in themselves. Catholic teaching maintains that some things are intrinsically and therefore always morally evil, even when circumstances excuse one from moral guilt. It may seem like splitting hairs, but it seems to me that the situationist approach to moral decision-making blinds us to the tragic dimension of life. If our actions are "good" and not simply "evil but excusable," we relieve ourselves of the burden of having to choose evil in order to avoid a greater evil. It was tragic that the Frankls felt they had to abort their unborn child. It is tragic that killing is sometimes the lesser of two evils. It is tragic that people must sometimes lie to save the innocent or steal to stay alive. If we blind ourselves to this tragedy by labelling these actions as "good," do we then blind ourselves to the need to change a world in which such tragedies exist?

By way of clarification, we might conclude by asking this simple question: How does a Catholic, confronted by the moral teachings of the Church, exercise that freedom of conscience which the Church itself considers everyone's right and duty (*Catechism of the Catholic Church* #1790)? My answer would be that, in the context of Catholic morality, there are three requirements for a free moral decision.

1. As noted in Chapter 7, freedom of conscience is not simply freedom to do as one pleases, but freedom to act according to one's own deeply held values and convictions. This means that Catholics can only combine freedom with living according to Catholic moral values when they have made those moral values their own. Only then does morality become a matter of integrity, of being true to oneself and therefore free. As noted above (p. 109), the moral teachings of the Church are aimed at those who have made such a moral commitment. For those who have rejected those teachings there is no conflict.

2. As already stated, freedom of conscience must include the freedom to decide when something objectively or intrinsically evil might, in a given set of circumstances, be the lesser of two

evils and, therefore, morally permissible. In other words, something intrinsically evil (killing, lying, stealing, etc.) might not necessarily be a sin in certain circumstances. To make this distinction between "evil" and "sin" is simply to restate the traditional distinction that moralists make between "material sin" and "formal sin." Material sin refers to the "matter" of the act (the killing, lying, etc.), considered in itself and apart from the circumstances and the intention of the one acting. The concept of formal sin recognizes that sin is a personal, subjective act requiring full knowledge and consent and carried out in a particular set of circumstances. Our distinction could then be stated as follows: Something that is objectively (materially) sinful may not be subjectively (formally) sinful. Since, however, sin is by definition something personal and subjective (involving personal will and decision), I find it confusing to speak of "objective" or "material" sin. It is less confusing, I believe, to distinguish "sin" (a personal act or omission) from "evil" (an objective value judgment).

3. Finally, moral decisions are not truly free unless one sincerely tries to do what is objectively right. Even in particular circumstances there is an objectively true solution to the moral dilemma, even though one may never arrive at that solution with absolute certainty. As noted above (p. 109), many moral and life decisions cannot be made with the absolute certainty of being right. One can only follow one's conscience with sincere good faith. According to Church teaching, this kind of good faith requires that such decisions be made by an "informed" conscience. For a committed Catholic, this means informing oneself about the teaching of the Church as it applies to one's particular moral dilemma. It might also mean seeking moral or spiritual guidance or divine help through prayer. In some cases it might mean seeking medical advice or professional counselling. It also involves careful scrutiny of one's past experience and present circumstances as well as the possible consequences of one's decision. After all this, however, one still has to make a free and responsible decision. Informing one's conscience by consulting authority does not mean letting the authority make the decision for you. It is a way of assuring that one's freely made decision is also a responsible one.

# 9. DO WE NEED THE CHURCH?

A newspaper article of Oct. 1, 1997,[39] describes pre-Vatican II Catholics as follows: "Catholics declared themselves symbolically (no meat on Fridays, the crucifix often prominently worn) and lived by Church-written rules. Divorce was unthinkable. Birth control was a sin (abortion wasn't even discussed). Catholics worshipped in Latin." The article goes on to state that all this changed with the convening of Vatican II in 1962. Now Catholics felt free to discuss Church doctrine and moral teachings. "Soon it became difficult to know what Catholicism meant or what the Church intended to be." I am sure that many Catholics would agree with this assessment of the recent history of their Church. There is no doubt that in a general way it accurately describes a certain loss of Catholic identity since Vatican II. And yet I find it misleading in at least two ways. First, "Church-written rules" were never the ultimate criteria for Catholics in making moral decisions. As we have seen, when the *Catechism of the Catholic Church* insists that "a human being must always obey the certain judgment of his conscience" (#1790), it reiterates a principle of freedom of conscience that has always been a staple of Catholic moral teaching. Second, it is inaccurate to say that birth control – or anything else, for that matter – is a "sin." The Church's moral teachings are concerned with identifying what is "morally evil" in an objective sense: that is, considering only the act itself and abstracting from the concrete circumstances and the intention of the individual. In those concrete circumstances it is the individual conscience that must decide whether what is "morally evil" is also a "sin," an offence against God and one's conscience. Any other conclusion renders the statement of the Catechism unintelligible.

If this is true, whence comes the idea that being a Catholic means obedience to the "rules" of the Church, which decide for us what is a sin and what isn't? In other words, that the rules are seen as making our moral decisions for us? Perhaps it is because

---

[39] Robert Fulford, "News media blind to spiritual side of Catholicism," *The Globe and Mail,* Oct. 1, 1997.

for most Catholics, particularly in the pre-Vatican II Church, the Church's teaching on freedom of conscience was – put as gently as possible – somewhat muted. Most Catholics of pre-Vatican II vintage will have to be excused for regarding the principle of freedom of conscience as a well-kept secret. These are what I call "perplexed" Catholics: they labour under a false, distorted understanding of their religion. If there was a failure on the part of the Church, it was a failure to educate, to form mature consciences by allowing people to continue in the belief that their moral lives did not involve personal responsibility and the freedom that must accompany such responsibility. But the failure is not always one-sided. Lots of folks are only too willing to be told what to do and refuse to take responsibility for their own decisions. It would be naive to think that the distortions and legalisms of the past are no longer a factor in the post-Vatican II Church. It is clear that more than 30 years after Vatican II many Catholics are still unable to resolve conflicts between individual conscience and Church teaching.

The failure to resolve this kind of conflict is, I believe, at the root of the alienation from the Church that many Catholics feel. As a result, many have simply opted out of the Church. They perceive the moral teachings of the Church as demanding an unthinking obedience that conflicts with their freedom of conscience and their personal relationship with God. They have not necessarily abandoned the faith. In many cases they are Catholics without a Church, pursuing a personal relationship with God and trying to live a good moral life apart from Church moral teaching and worship. This raises some questions: Can one live a Catholic Christian life without participating in the life of the Church? Isn't it possible to live a good life, to love God and one's neighbour apart from the dogma and ritual of the Church? In other words, do we really need the Church?

This question parallels the question asked in Chapter 1: Is religion necessary? There I suggested that, simply from the point of view of satisfying our spiritual needs or fulfilling spiritual values, religion need not be considered necessary. As Christians, however, our religion derives its "necessity" from the fact that it is not simply a means of satisfying an inner human and spiritual need; it is a response to a revelation and to a call from beyond the self, from a transcendent God. Moreover, the Christian response to God's self-revelation in Christ is faith. To summarize what has already been said about faith, when one responds to the Christian message with faith one makes a radical act of trust in God's love as revealed in Christ; it is a trusting acceptance of God's love. The result is liberation from the oppression of "the law," from the necessity of earning that love and acceptance. It is this assurance of God's freely given love and acceptance that frees the Christian from excessive self-preoccupation in the form of concern over our worthiness and acceptability. The psychological effect of such freedom from self is the freedom to be concerned about others and their needs. There is a necessary connection then between faith and love. The less preoccupied I am with myself, the freer I am to be for others and to love others.

Thus, the Christian message and the response of faith are not merely intended to give each believer a warm, fuzzy feeling of being loved and accepted. They are intended to heal our sense of alienation from ourselves and the world around us. They are intended to open us up to the people around us, to enable us to reach out with concern for their needs and problems. If faith makes possible (to some degree at least) this kind of self-transcending love and concern for others, then it makes possible some kind of genuine human community. We may say that the ultimate purpose of the experience of grace and faith is to create a community of love, unity and solidarity. This community, in turn, serves as a sign to the world at large of the kind of community that humanity is trying to achieve. The response of faith to God's grace involves being part of this community of faith and therefore of love. This community of love is what the Church is supposed to be. The reader may wish to pause here for a moment of cynical reflection on the cliques, petty jealousies and lack of community feeling that sometimes blemish the life of parish communities and that make it difficult to think of these as communities of love. And yet when we think of all our human attempts at love – romantic, conjugal, parental and fraternal – of how flawed they are and of how short of their ideals they fall, should we be surprised that the Church falls so short of the ideal of being a community of love?

# III. The Moral Life

It is important to remember that the Church, like any other human community, organizes and structures itself. It becomes an institution complete with a bureaucracy that administers, organizes and makes rules governing the life of the Church. We should not be surprised when this administrative structure sometimes displays typical bureaucratic pettiness and lack of vision. At the same time, it is important to differentiate between this visible, structured, organized aspect of the Church and the spiritual reality of the community of faith; between the Church as institution and the Church as community. We baptized Catholics make up this community and, therefore, we are the Church. The *Catechism of the Catholic Church* emphasizes this twofold aspect of the Church as both a visible and a spiritual reality. The Church is described as a society structured with hierarchical organs and the mystical body of Christ; the visible society and the spiritual community; the earthly Church and the Church endowed with heavenly riches (#771). It is only with the eyes of faith, the Catechism states, that "one can see her in her visible reality and at the same time in her spiritual reality as bearer of divine life" (#770). Many perplexed Catholics have left the Church because they could not see the "bearer of divine life" in what appeared to be such a flawed human institution. While respecting their decision, I would like to offer some thoughts on the meaning of the Church and its role in our lives.

The Catechism, following the teachings of Vatican II, stresses the fact that the Church's function is to be "the sacrament of the inner union of men with God" (#775). We know that a sacrament is a "visible sign of grace," a visible reality (the bread and wine of the Eucharist, the water of baptism, the oil of confirmation, etc.) that is a sign of the inner spiritual reality of God's redeeming love. Christ can be regarded as the sacrament of God because, in his visible, tangible reality, he reveals in a visible human way the invisible God. The Church in turn can be regarded as the sacrament of Christ since, in its visible, tangible reality, it reveals the love of Christ and carries forward his saving work. The Church, therefore, as the Catechism notes, has no meaning and function apart from Christ. Its only task is to carry on the work of Christ and to faithfully transmit his message of salvation to the world. As the Catechism puts it: "The Church has no other light than Christ's;

115

according to a favorite image of the Church fathers, the Church is like the moon, all its light reflected from the sun" (#748).

Any serious criticism of the Church should therefore be based on the criterion of its true function. The Church should be measured by the standard of whether or not it is faithfully proclaiming the message of Christ and living by the values of the Gospel. Simple-minded calls for the Church to "keep up with the times" are using a false standard of judgment. (In fact, historically, the Church has more often than not been well ahead of the times, especially in the fields of education, care of the sick and marginalized, and social justice.) Our understanding of the Church and its function should embrace both of its aspects: the Church as visible institution and as community of faith.

1. *The Church as visible institution.* There was a time when Catholics acknowledged the teaching and nurturing function of the Church by referring to the Church as our spiritual "mother." In these "enlightened" times, however, the phrase "Holy Mother the Church" seems to have been abandoned. Perhaps this phrase suggests an obstacle to our desire for autonomy: that in the Church we remain, even in adulthood, obedient children of a mother figure. And yet, properly understood, it is a beautiful way of understanding our relationship to the Church and, paradoxically, the freedom and autonomy we enjoy as Christians. Of course there are those who fail to outgrow their infantile dependence on their mother and look to the Church to be a mother substitute who will do for them what mother rightly did for them when they were little children – provide them with unconditional love, certainty and security, shelter them from the harsh realities of life, comfort them and make their decisions for them. To turn the Church into this kind of a mother substitute is surely a distortion of the image of the Church as mother and contrary to everything we know about genuine motherhood. The Church is not intended to be a mother substitute who, even when we are adults, continues to do our thinking for us and make our decisions for us; she is intended to be a mother symbol who performs the function of a good mother by allowing and encouraging us to grow up and become mature Christian adults.

In the normal course of development, mother is the bridge we cross in order to encounter the world. To be sure, as the child's first love object, she provides the love, certainty and security that allow the child to develop trust and self-confidence. Trust in mother is the foundation for developing trust in oneself, or self-confidence. This attitude of trust and self-confidence is in turn the foundation for the child's growing sense of autonomy and independence. In time, this becomes a sense of self-awareness, personal identity and the ability to think and decide and be responsible for oneself. The good mother fosters and encourages this growing sense of autonomy and personal responsibility. As a result, the ties of dependency are severed. The child learns to look beyond the mother's emotional orbit to the world and to form bonds of love and solidarity with others. As a further result, when the child becomes an adult, the mother-child relationship changes from one of dependency to something closer to love between equals, from one-sided dependency to mutuality. It may even happen that in mother's old age the roles of mother and child are reversed and the adult child becomes the caregiver for the now dependent mother.

What does all this suggest about the role of the Church as a "spiritual mother"? In his book *Freud and Christianity,* R.S. Lee writes: "The Church takes over in religious development the functions of the mother and does so in a real sense psychologically." Therefore, he concludes, "the good Church must have the same characteristics as the good family mother."[40] In other words, the Church, like any good mother, should allow her children to grow up into responsible adult Christians. As Lee puts it, "The Church should treat her children in the way equivalent to that of the mother who sets her children free of infantile bondage to herself." The Church should not see her function "as that of imposing her authority over her members, of disciplining them, of prescribing how they must behave, of giving them rules of belief and conduct that they must not question."[41] The function of the Church is not to bind her children to herself like a possessive mother, but to be for them a

---

[40] *Freud and Christianity* (Harmondsworth, England: Penguin Books, 1967), pp. 111-112.

[41] Freud and Christianity, p. 111.

bridge to reality: the ultimate reality of God and his love for us as revealed in Christ.

What, then, is the authority of the Church in our moral and religious lives? It is the authority of a mother and, as with our biological or adoptive mothers, our attitude towards that authority is subject to change and development. As little children, our attitude is one of obedience to mother's rules. Our sole moral criterion is what is "allowed" and what is "not allowed." As we mature we outgrow that kind of obedience and learn to be responsible for our own decisions, moral or otherwise. As adults, however, we may well discover that we are living by the same values that were the basis of mother's rules. What has happened is that we have internalized and made our own the values we were taught by another. These values have now become our own and the motivation to live by them comes from within ourselves and not from mother or any other outside source. Mature Catholics follow a similar path of development. The values they live by are the values they learned from their spiritual mother the Church, initially by way of "rules." But they have made these values their own personal values, and living by them has become a matter of integrity, of being true to themselves and their own freely chosen values. The moral teachings of the Church are no longer seen as rules imposed upon people, but as a set of values that they have adopted as their own and in the context of which they must make responsible moral decisions.

If some Catholics are "perplexed" it is in part because they think (or have been led to think) that being a Catholic means obeying rules rather than being guided by values. Obeying rules, however, is the morality of a child. The moral teaching of the Church is intended to help free and responsible adults to make moral decisions, not to make our moral decisions for us. Individual consciences must apply the values taught by the Church to the concrete circumstances of life. For example, the Church teaches the value of every human life. Yet killing, though always remaining objectively evil, can be excusable in certain circumstances, as the Church itself acknowledges. What is less readily admitted is that, having looked to the Church for guidance, the individual conscience must decide when such an exception is to be made. Those who reduce the moral guidance of the Church to a set of concrete rules to be blindly obeyed often seem to believe that they are taking the moral high road. In fact, they are taking the easy way out by evading their personal moral responsibility.

2. *The Church as community*. The Church as a visible society is a "sacrament." It is meant to give visible expression to the spiritual community of faith, love and unity. This visible expression is never perfect; it can only be, even at the best of times, an approximation of that spiritual reality. It cannot fully express the "mystery" it reveals. As a spiritual reality, therefore, the Church can only understand its inner nature by using various images and metaphors. The *Catechism of the Catholic Church* lists three of those images as pre-eminent: the Church is the "people of God," the "body of Christ" and the "bride of Christ."

What do these three images tell us about the nature of the Church and especially about the meaning of our membership in the Church? Since being part of a community emphasizes the social dimension of life, I would like to put our discussion into the context of what the great social psychologist Alfred Adler (1870–1937) had to say about the social meaning of life. His thoughts on this subject might help us to understand the social nature of the Church and of the Christian life. Adler believed that we all begin life with "feelings of inferiority." Throughout life we try to compensate for these feelings by striving for superiority. The critical question is this: Do we strive to be superior in an egocentric way that has no meaning for others (not really to be superior but merely to feel superior) or do we strive to be superior in a way that involves being "useful," in a way that involves making a contribution to the welfare of human life and the human community? Adler refers to the former as giving a "private meaning" to life and to the latter as giving a "social meaning" to life or having "social interest." Maturity is measured by one's degree of social interest.

There are three areas of life, Adler believes, that challenge us to give a social meaning to life. These are occupation, social life, and love and marriage. By observing how a person responds to the challenges of these three "problem areas" of life, we can determine the degree of social interest in that person's lifestyle.

That lifestyle reveals to what extent a person gives life a private ("useless") meaning or a social ("useful") meaning. Is one's work an opportunity to make a worthwhile contribution to society? Is one's social life of genuine concern for others? Is one's love life one of intimate and many-sided co-operation? If so, one will see life as a "creative task." To such a person "life means to be interested in my fellow-man, to be part of the whole, to contribute my share to the welfare of mankind."[42] This view that life finds its meaning and completion in commitment to others challenges the attitude of those who see life as a self-absorbed pursuit of "self-actualization" unrelated to others. It also challenges the religious attitude that sees life as a relentless pursuit of moral and religious "perfection" or "merit" or "virtue" or one's own salvation.

Adler's "problem areas" of life – work, social life, and love and marriage – pretty much make up the "stuff" of the average person's life. If these three areas of life have a social meaning, then I believe that our membership in the Church – understood as the people of God, the body of Christ and the bride of Christ – gives a more ultimate dimension to that social meaning.

1. *People of God*. The Catechism tells us that the destiny of the people of God is the realization of the "kingdom of God" (#782). The Christian "awaits" (as the creed says) and hopes for the coming of God's kingdom, which is the ultimate state of love, peace, unity and solidarity, as well as the ultimate victory over death, of which Christ's resurrection is seen as a pledge. In the words of the preface for the feast of Christ the King, the Christian hopes for "a kingdom of truth and life, a kingdom of holiness and grace, a kingdom of justice, love and peace." The task of the Church, as the people of God, is to communicate this hope to the world by embodying in its own communal life some partial realization of the life of the kingdom that is to come. As Pope John Paul II writes: "Being Christians in our day means being builders of communion in the Church and in society" (*Slavorum Apostoli*, 27). When the Pharisees asked Jesus when the kingdom of God was to come, he replied, "The kingdom of God is among you" (Luke 17:21), since he himself was the

---

[42] *What Life Should Mean to You* (New York: Capricorn Books, 1958), pp. 7-8.

embodiment of that kingdom. As the visible "sacrament" of Christ, the Church also strives to be an embodiment of that life of "justice, love and peace," which it believes to be the ultimate destiny of the whole human community. Every instance of injustice, enmity and discord in the Church is a betrayal of that function. On more than one occasion, Pope John Paul II has asked the world's forgiveness for the Church's past failures in this regard.

The Church's obvious failures, however, do not alter the fact that individual Christians are called to co-operate with God in working to bring about the realization of God's kingdom both in their personal lives and in the world. Christians carry out this task in large part through the contribution they make to the life of the human community. In this light their daily occupation takes on an eternal significance. It is not just a means of earning a living or even of contributing to the current well-being of society. It is also a contribution to the ultimate well-being of the human community: the kingdom of God. From the perspective of faith, even the most humble work has religious and eternal significance. For this reason the Church has always insisted on the dignity of work as such and does not share the view that only work that is perceived as "meaningful" from a human perspective is of value. It is this "theology of work" that lies behind the practice of many devout Catholics (is it still a practice?) of offering their life and work to God at Sunday Mass as part of the sacrifice that is offered. The implied prayer is that God will take their work and make it fruitful just as Jesus once accepted some loaves and fish from a young boy and did something wonderful with them.

2. *Body of Christ*. "Just as each of our bodies," writes St. Paul, "has several parts and each part has a separate function, so all of us, in union with Christ, form one body, and as parts of it, we belong to each other" (Romans 12:4-5). Christ and the Christian community together constitute a "body" in which Christ is the head and we are the members of the body. What does this image say about life "in Christ"? First, it implies that our lives are lived "in union with Christ," under the direction of Christ's teaching and example, just as the activity of the body is co-ordinated by the head. Christians are to think, speak and act

as Christ would. "In your minds," St. Paul writes, "you must be the same as Christ Jesus" (Philippians 2:5). Second, the union of each believer with Christ implies union among the believers. They "belong to each other" as members of the same body. Third, each member or organ of the body has a unique function to perform that contributes to the overall welfare of the body. In the same way, each of us has unique gifts to bring to the life and work of the Church. The unique contributions of all the members, writes St. Paul, "are all the work of one and the same Spirit who distributes different gifts to different people as he chooses" (1 Corinthians 12:11). Fourth, the union of all with Christ overrides all distinctions of race, nationality, gender and social condition, for in Christ "there is neither Jew nor Greek, there is neither slave nor free, there is neither male nor female" (Galatians 3:28). Finally, the union of all in Christ creates a special bond of empathy among the members so that "If one part is hurt, all parts are hurt with it" and "if one part is given special honour, all parts enjoy it" (1 Corinthians 12:26).

The identification of the Church as the body of Christ implies that in one's social relationships we are relating in some sense to Christ himself, as one member of Christ's body to another. This in turn gives an ultimate religious meaning to the believer's interpersonal and communal life, to that dimension of life that Adler calls the area of social co-operation. The doctrine of the body of Christ implies that if Christ is to be found in the world, it is only in his visible body: in the human face of one's neighbour. "I tell you solemnly," Christ says to us, "insofar as you did it to one of the least of these brothers of mine, you did it to me" (Matthew 25:40). To serve Christ is to serve him in his sometimes all too human members. This concern for the very earthly needs of our fellow human beings who make up the body of Christ is what Adler calls social interest.

3. *Bride of Christ.* In Christian tradition the relationship between Christ and the Church is viewed as a kind of "marriage" in which the Church is the bride and Christ is the bridegroom. In this respect it is a continuation of the Old Testament view where the covenant between God and his chosen people is viewed as a marriage contract and the people's failure to live up to the demands of that covenant (e.g., worshipping false gods)

constitutes a kind of adultery or infidelity. Speaking on God's behalf, the prophet Jeremiah rebukes the people for their sins in these words: "Like a woman faithless to her lover, even so have you been faithless to me" (Jeremiah 3:20). It is for this reason that the Church regards marriage as a sacrament. The union of husband and wife is meant to be a visible, "sacramental" sign of the union of Christ the bridegroom and his bride the Church. In their love, the love between Christ and the Church is meant to become a visible reality. Adler speaks of marriage as an area of life that challenges us to give a social rather than a private meaning to life. For a marriage to succeed, individualism and self-preoccupation have to be outgrown; one has to think and act as part of a couple. To this psychological meaning of marriage the Church adds a theological and more ultimate meaning: marriage is a sacrament in which the love of Christ and his Church is made visible. For this reason the Church, in the marriage ceremony, urges the bride and groom to go beyond an intimate love affair between two people oblivious to the rest of the world (though it may indeed begin that way) and to strive for a love that, like the love of Christ, reaches out to the world and its needs. In the final blessing of the bride and groom, the priest prays: "May you always bear witness to the love of God in this world so that the afflicted and the needy will find in you generous friends and welcome you into the joys of heaven."

Christianity is not just about our personal faith relationship with God. It is about the building of community – the community of believers that is the Church and ultimately the building up of the community of humankind. As we grow towards a mature faith, our focus becomes less a matter of obedience to "Mother Church" and more a matter of responsible participation in the community of faith. Our participation in the life of the Church gives to our lives not just the social meaning of which Adler speaks, but an ultimate social meaning. And yet, even as our focus shifts from the motherly institution to the community of which we are a part and for which we are responsible, the Church always remains, in some sense, our "mother." For the average person, the relationship to mother in the course of one's growing up is not simple and uncomplicated. To be sure, mother is the source of life, love, comfort and security. And yet there are times when she can be an object of resentment and rebellion, a source of embarrassment or an obstacle to one's growing need for independence. Should we be surprised that we sometimes have these same conflicting feelings towards the Church as our spiritual mother? And yet, as mother ages, the children who once needed her care and protection discover that it is mother who now needs their care and protection. Some have found it necessary to leave the Church, just as some children find it necessary to leave home. For others, however, their attachment to the Church is rooted not so much in a need for the Church and its authority as in the conviction that the Church needs them. The Church we call mother is like any mother; it is her children who keep her young.

# PART IV

# THE MEANING OF SALVATION

What do Christians mean when they talk about salvation? What are they saved from and how is that salvation accomplished? So far we have tried to answer those two questions only in reference to our present earthly life. One is saved from sin (the human condition of alienation and separation) by the grace of God received in faith. But this is only a partial realization of the goal of salvation. In this section we want to look at the meaning of salvation in terms of its ultimate goal and completion. To do so it is important to at least attempt to answer three questions:

1) In what sense is Jesus Christ "saviour" or the author of salvation?

2) How do the sacraments continue the saving work of Christ?

3) What can we know about the ultimate goal of the process of salvation, "eternal life"?

## 10. WHO IS JESUS CHRIST?

Once, when teaching a university course in Religious Studies, I had occasion to mention the concern among some Christians for some kind of certainty or assurance of salvation. At this point a student asked, "Salvation from what?" I was reminded of the old story about the zealot who spray-painted the wall of a subway with the words "Jesus is the answer!" Underneath this message another spray-painter asked, "What was the question?" In our reflections to this point, we have tried to answer the questions "salvation from what" and "how" by trying to unpack the human experiences represented by the words "sin," "grace" and "faith." Christians believe they are saved from the state of sin (the condition of separation or estrangement from self, others and God) by God's grace (unconditional love) and their trusting belief in that love (faith). This salvation or healing, which is experienced in a partial and fragmentary way in this life, will be experienced in all its fullness in eternity.

Christians also believe that their salvation is somehow accomplished by the life, death and resurrection of Jesus Christ. Hence he is referred to as "saviour" or "redeemer." Moreover, he is qualified to be saviour and redeemer since, as the Roman centurion who witnessed his death and its aftermath confessed, "Truly, this was the son of God" (Matthew 27:54). But what does it mean to say that Jesus is the "Son of God"? As already noted in Chapter 3, for the early Christians, it seemed sufficient to know no more than this, to know Jesus as their saviour and redeemer, to understand what his life, death and resurrection meant for their human existence. As theological reflection developed, however, the question of what Jesus was in himself came to the fore. Did the fact that he was the Son of God mean that he was human or divine? If he was both, how are these two aspects united and reconciled? It was this kind of theological debate that necessitated the convening of ecumenical councils to define what the Church believed about such questions. The Council of Chalcedon in the year 451 provided the classic answer to the question about the nature of Christ. Jesus Christ, it taught, was one person possessing two natures: one fully human, the other fully divine. This, of course, was not a *rational* explanation of the mystery of Christ; it was a doctrinal formulation expressing the faith of the Church.

Like every other doctrinal formulation, it was a human attempt to explain the meaning of something that is essentially a mystery. As such, it is incomplete and subject to development. Consequently, the question of the "divinity of Christ" is a continuing topic not only of theological debate but also of popular fascination. If the reader has any doubts about this, I suggest the following experiment: write a letter to the editor of your local newspaper casting doubt on the divinity of Christ and expressing bewilderment at the naiveté of Christians who hold such an "irrational" belief. Then sit back and watch the letters of rebuttal pour in. And yet I am convinced that this question, like the question of the existence of God (see Chapter 3), is not the important question about Christ for those who have a mature Christian faith. Like the question of God's existence, it is a speculative question that engages the mind only; but faith is something beyond mind and rationality. No, the real question for the believer is still the "existential" question: What is the meaning of Jesus Christ for my life? The *religious* question about Jesus is the question of his *function* as saviour and redeemer. This more answerable question is less concerned with what the phrase "Son of God" tells us about the inner nature of Christ than about the salvation, atonement or reconciliation he brings about between God and ourselves.

It must be kept in mind that what the Church proposes for our belief is not a theological treatise on the nature of Christ but the Christian message of salvation. That message is transmitted by the teaching and preaching of the Church. That is why we include belief (the assent of the mind) among the elements of faith along with trust and moral commitment. The Acts of the Apostles describes the first Christians – those who accepted the preaching of the apostles and joined the Christian community – as "believers" (4:4; 13:12; 14:1; 15:5). The faith professed by that community held that Jesus was the Messiah, the Son of God (Matthew 16:16); that he delivered them through his death and resurrection from sin (1 Corinthians 15:16-17);

that he justified them through the gift of his Spirit (Romans 8:8-11); and that he communicates new life to baptized believers (Romans 6:4-5). We, too, who are members of the Church, are constituted as a community by our common faith in that same message of salvation. We profess this faith that we hold in common when we recite the creed together at Mass. At the same time, though we recite it as a group, we generally use the first person ("I believe"), reminding ourselves that each of us assimilates the faith of the community by a free and personal act of faith. (Whoever is responsible for translating the "Nicene" version of the creed in the plural – "*We* believe in one God" – seems to have overlooked this fact.)

When they recite the creed, what do Christians profess to believe about Jesus Christ? They believe that he is the "only Son" of "God the Father almighty"; that the Virgin Mary conceived and gave birth to him "by the power of the Holy Spirit"; that he was crucified, died and was buried and rose from the dead "on the third day"; that he ascended into heaven and will "come again to judge the living and the dead"; that because of all this, they have received the Holy Spirit, the forgiveness of sins, and eternal life. If one can recite this creed with conviction, there is no question that one's faith is "orthodox." At the same time, it is clear that different believers may have different interpretations of certain articles of the creed and yet these interpretations may all be faithful to the essential meaning of the Christian message. Church doctrine is usually stated in a way that allows for a certain amount of theological speculation. Two believers, for instance, may both profess their faith in a God who is the "creator of heaven and earth" and yet hold radically different views on how that creation was carried out. The scope of orthodoxy has room for both "creationists" and "evolutionists." Those who insist that their particular take on doctrinal questions is the one expected of all Catholics provide us with another distressing example of being "more Catholic than the pope." What can be said about the interpretation of doctrine in general is true of the question we are dealing with in this chapter – the meaning of Jesus Christ for our human existence, the meaning of terms such as saviour and redeemer as they apply to Christ. Faith maintains that Jesus Christ brought about the salvation of humanity through his life, death and resurrection. But exactly in what way is this true? How does the death of Christ bring about salvation? Here is where strict doctrine ends and theological speculation begins. Historically, there have been three main types of theological interpretation or theories that attempt to explain how Christ brought about the atonement, how he reunited or made "at one" God and humanity.[43]

1. *The ransom theory*. According to this theory, the saving work of Christ consists in liberating us from domination from alien powers that produce death. Hence the term "saviour" is the most apt term to describe Christ. The alien power in question may be variously described. Some would see this alien power as Satan, in which case salvation would be seen as liberation from the power of Satan and adoption as a child of God. The alien power might also be seen as sin, conceived of as a force dominating human existence. We have seen how St. Paul experienced sin in this way – as a power dominating his life, causing him to act contrary to his better judgment and frustrating his attempts to justify himself before God. In this view, salvation is perceived as deliverance from this kind of inner dividedness or conflict. A more contemporary view might conceive of this alien power as all powers alien to the ego: our unconscious, anti-social, destructive impulses. People who attribute their recovery from a serious alcohol or drug addiction to a religious conversion might be sympathetic to this view of salvation.

2. *The satisfaction theory*. In this view of the atonement Jesus becomes, as it were, a vicarious criminal. By his death he takes our place and is punished for our sins, making "satisfaction" for them, and thus saves us from the consequences of sin. The satisfaction theory portrays a God who is judge and lawgiver and who is both just and merciful. His justice demands that satisfaction or restitution be made; in his mercy, he sacrifices his Son to make satisfaction for humanity's sins. Only the death of this divine Son is seen as sufficient to make satisfaction and obtain forgiveness for sins that have offended God's divine sovereignty. In the satisfaction theory salvation is seen to consist essentially in the forgiveness of sins.

---

[43] For a summary of these three theories see Paul Pruyser, *A Dynamic Psychology of Religion* (New York: Harper & Row, 1968), pp. 317-328.

3. *The moral influence theory*. In this theory the saving work of Christ is seen as restoring to us the image of God in which the human person was created, but that has been defaced or obscured by sin. Here Christ is not seen so much as a sacrificial victim making satisfaction for sin, but more as one who reveals the goodness of God and thereby gives us an example to follow. As Paul Pruyser puts it, "Christ identifies himself with man out of sympathy and mercy, whatever his function towards God might be, and this has the moral effect of making man desire to identify himself with Christ, his life, his teachings and his perfection."[44] Salvation, then, is seen as being brought about through one's identification with Christ.

How are these theories of salvation or atonement to be evaluated, especially with regard to their ability to speak meaningfully to today's Christians? Pruyser finds psychological significance in each of the three types of atonement theory by pointing out that each theory is relevant to a particular type of psychological or "intrapsychic" conflict that, according to psychoanalytic theory, we experience in our human life. The ransom theory relates to the kind of conflicts we experience between the ego (the rational, problem-solving dimension of personality) and the id (the reservoir of unsatisfied instinctual impulses) in which the rational ego feels itself to be captive to the irrational impulses of the id. The satisfaction theory speaks to the anxiety experienced by the ego in its conflicts with the demanding and forbidding superego (the internalized voice of the commands and prohibitions of authority figures). In other words, it relates to our experience of guilt. The moral influence theory, with its emphasis on identification with Christ as a model to be followed, represents a desire to become one's better or ideal self. It is relevant, therefore, to the ongoing conflict experienced between the ego (the actual self) and the ego-ideal (the ideal self). The motivating factor here is not so much guilt, as in the satisfaction theory, but the shame one feels at falling short of this ideal.

What is important to remember is that one's belief in the Church's doctrine of atonement is not a commitment to an exclusive acceptance or understanding of any one of these

---

[44] *A Dynamic Psychology of Religion*, p. 321.

theories of how atonement is accomplished. The late Christian apologist Malcolm Muggeridge claimed to be "absolutely indifferent" to the details of the resurrection story ("whether the stone was moved or not moved, or what anybody saw, or anything like that"). Nor did he consider the question of the virgin birth "of any importance." For him, the important thing about Jesus is "that he lived and lives."[45] Now this kind of talk might seem a bit too flippant to the sensibilities of some Christians. Nevertheless, Muggeridge's attitude is instructive. It reminds us that an essential Christian doctrine should not be exclusively identified with one theological interpretation of that doctrine. It is important to separate the essential from the non-essential. Most Catholics do this up to a point. They know, for instance, that it is not really important to their faith whether the Virgin Mary really appeared to St. Bernadette or to the children at Fatima, or whether the shroud of Turin is really the burial shroud of Christ. One's faith does not depend on such things. And yet there is a kind of religious instruction that leads Christians to believe that a particular interpretation of Christian doctrine – the satisfaction theory of atonement, for example – is essential to their faith. But the doctrine of atonement is not restricted to one interpretation; a rejection of one theological interpretation is not a denial of the essential doctrine.

Note, for example, that when Malcolm Muggeridge asserts that the details of the resurrection story or the idea of the virgin birth are not matters "of any importance" to him, he is not denying the resurrection or the virgin birth. It is all a matter of perspective, of distinguishing what is more important from what is less important. Most of us can distinguish between doctrines that we believe but that are not very relevant to our daily lives and doctrines that truly give meaning and purpose to our everyday life and thought. This should not be surprising. For devout Catholics, doctrines such as God's loving providence or the real presence of Christ in the Eucharist may be fundamental to their lives, while doctrines such as the Immaculate Conception or the Assumption remain dormant. On this same basis one might differentiate between the various

---

[45] *Jesus Rediscovered* (London: Hodder and Stoughton, 1995, c. 1969), pp. 164-167.

theories of atonement. Each may contain elements of meaningful truth for individual believers. Each may offer a fruitful way of understanding the meaning of Jesus' death and resurrection for different believers. But none are definitive or authoritative and each may have its shortcomings. Contemporary Christians, for example, might find the God of the satisfaction theory who demands the death of his son as atonement for offences against him far too harsh and demanding. The ransom theory – especially when presented as a victory over and liberation from Satan – may strike some as too simplistic and unsophisticated in its understanding of the evil forces that dominate our human existence. The moral influence theory, which presents Jesus as an example to be followed, seems to strip Jesus' cross of any saving or redemptive meaning. If Christians are left to imitate Jesus through their own human resources, they may be trying to justify themselves before God – trying to earn salvation – which is an obstacle to faith (see Chapter 5).

And yet each of these three ways of experiencing the atonement wrought by Christ has its own particular appeal, for the simple reason that the condition of sin from which we are saved is experienced in different ways. This condition of estrangement from my true, total and better self, from my fellow human beings, and ultimately from God gives rise to all three types of feelings: feelings of enslavement, guilt and shame. Nor does one need to be religious to have such feelings. To those who feel entrapped and dominated by some form of evil so that they act contrary to their ideals and convictions, contrary to their "true" self, the image of Christ as saviour who liberates them from this overpowering influence is appealing. St. Paul experienced sin in this way (Romans 7). To one who experiences the guilt that follows from the condition of sin (we are not speaking here of neurotic "guilt feelings"), the image of Christ the redeemer standing in for the sinners, as it were, and suffering the consequences of sin on their behalf can be a fruitful way of understanding the expiatory nature of Christ's death. In the Catholic tradition this has given rise, in popular piety, to the notion of vicarious suffering: that suffering or negative experiences generally can be "offered up" for the benefit of others – the "souls in purgatory" being the usual beneficiaries of choice. Today, this practice does not seem to be widespread and we tend to look back skeptically at this kind of piety. And yet, as someone has remarked, it is still difficult to think of anything better to say to a 10-year-old on the way to the dentist. Finally, the image of Christ restoring the divine image to a fallen humanity through his identification with the human condition and human example can be motivating for those whose primary experience of sin is the shame of estrangement from their ideal self. Amidst the failure of one's idealism, Christ becomes a divine role model.

In the liturgy of the Church, the mystery of salvation has traditionally been proclaimed using all three of these images of atonement. And in the most solemn liturgy of all, the Easter Vigil on Holy Saturday night, which culminates in the first Easter Mass, all these images of atonement are mentioned in the "*Exsultet.*" This magnificent hymn in praise of the salvation wrought by Christ is chanted after the lighting of the Easter (Paschal) candle. Here we are reminded that Christ "ransomed us with his blood" (ransom theory) and "paid for us the price of Adam's sin to our eternal Father" (satisfaction theory). On this night we commemorate the fact that God "freed the people of Israel from their slavery," foreshadowing our own liberation from sin (ransom theory). It is "the night when Christians everywhere, washed clean of sin and freed from all defilement, are restored to grace and grow together in holiness" (restoration of God's image in us). We are then invited to marvel at God's "merciful love," since "to ransom a slave you gave away your Son" (ransom theory). The "power of this holy night dispels all evil, washes away guilt, restores lost innocence, brings mourners joy" (satisfaction theory). The hymn concludes with a prayer that the Easter candle will continue to burn and dispel "the darkness of the night" as a symbol of Christ "who came back from the dead and shed his peaceful light on all mankind" (moral influence theory).

It is clear that the mystery of Christ and the salvation he accomplished cannot be fully comprehended in one simple human image. All images and metaphors used to describe the salvation wrought by Christ suffer from the same incompleteness as our human images of God. The question I should like the reader to ponder, however, is this: Can we arrive at an understanding of Jesus Christ and the atonement he brought about in a way that is consistent with the meaning of sin, grace and faith as proposed in this book? It has been suggested that salvation is accomplished, or the human condition of separation (sin) is healed, through the revelation of God's unconditional love (grace) and the human response of trusting belief in and acceptance of that love (faith). When faith is genuine, this love tends to transform the believers, to liberate them – as love always does – from self-absorption and lead them to greater concern for and openness to others. This process is true not only of growth in faith, but also of growth towards being fully human. Jean Vanier has described this process of "becoming human" very simply. It happens, he writes, when one is able to "receive love, be transformed by love, and then give love."[46] It should be obvious, then, that faith in some sense is critical to becoming both fully Christian and fully human; faith makes it possible for us to receive love (human or divine) and be transformed by it.

What I am suggesting is that salvation or atonement is to be understood as the transforming effect of God's love, which is revealed in the life, death and resurrection of Jesus Christ. Is there any theological justification for this view? If so, it begins with an understanding of Jesus as the one in whom God is revealed: more specifically, as the revelation of God's love or of the God who is Love. The Protestant theologian Dietrich Bonhoeffer emphasized this way of understanding Jesus when he referred to him as the "man for others." In the complete giving of himself to others, to the point of death, we see the love of God; we see what God would be like if he were human. To be like God, to "participate in the Being of God," means to be like Christ, to experience a "new life for others." This, for Bonhoeffer, was the meaning of "transcendence"; it was an experience of this new life for others that transcends our ordinary, all-too-human tendency towards a self-centred, self-absorbed way of life. From the Nazi prison camp in which he eventually died, Bonhoeffer wrote: "Our relation to God is not a religious relationship to a supreme Being, absolute in power and goodness, which is a spurious conception of transcendence, but

---

[46] *Becoming Human* (Toronto: Anansi Press, 1998), p. 23.

a new life for others, through participation in the Being of God." The God whom Christ reveals is found in human form, in a "man existing for others, and hence the Crucified."[47]

This last statement suggests that Bonhoeffer finds a necessary connection between Christ as the revelation of God's love and the cross. In his 1963 book, *Honest to God*, John A.T. Robinson (1919–1983), the Anglican bishop of Woolwich, England, tried to elaborate on the thoughts that Bonhoeffer did not have time to complete. In doing so, he asks us to rethink the oft-quoted words of St. Paul: "His [Jesus'] state was divine, yet he did not cling to his equality with God but *emptied himself*...even accepting death on a cross" (Philippians 2:6-8). What does it mean to say that Christ "emptied himself"? Christians have traditionally understood this in terms of God the Son stripping himself of his divine attributes (omnipotence, omniscience, etc.) in becoming a human being. Bishop Robinson, however, supports the view that it is the way Christ emptied himself "not of his Godhead but of himself, of any desire to focus attention on himself, of any craving to be 'on an equality with God' that he reveals God. For it is in making himself nothing, in his utter self-surrender to others in love, that he discloses and lays bare the Ground of man's being as Love."[48] Jesus has so emptied himself of egoism and self-seeking and has so focused on the needs and concerns of others that his life is a revelation of God's love for humanity. The cross is the ultimate expression of that love. This understanding of Jesus Christ and the atonement seems to be consistent with and to incorporate the other theories of atonement that we have reviewed. The love (grace) of God revealed in Christ is liberating in the sense that we are liberated from the need to constantly justify or prove ourselves (ransom theory). It is forgiving and thus removes the burden of guilt (satisfaction theory). It is transforming since it makes possible this new life for others (moral influence theory). This view recognizes that the love revealed in Christ is not merely a good example to be followed but, when received in faith, is truly transforming – as all genuine love is.

---

[47] *Letters and Papers from Prison* (London: S.C.M. Press, 1959), p. 165.

[48] Honest to God (London: S.C.M. Press, 1963), p. 75.

## 11. WHY DO WE HAVE SACRAMENTS ?

I once lived in a house that had a large bush in the backyard. By a certain point of the summer season the leaves of this bush turned a bright shade of red. I was so taken with the beauty of this bush that I used to refer to it – not altogether jokingly – as my "proof for the existence of God." I was not even aware of the plant's proper name until a friend informed me that it was called a "burning bush." A perfect name, I thought, since in that name I could see a reference not only to its red leaves but also to the bush in which God revealed himself to Moses (Exodus 3). Now, we know that finding God in nature is not uncommon. Many people, including many who are not religious in any conventional sense, find or experience God or at least something transcendent in the beauty of nature. They may also find the divine or transcendent in instances of humanly created beauty such as art, literature or music.

These experiences of beauty are usually referred to as "aesthetic" ones. I believe there are two different ways that we may encounter God in such experiences. First, we can use the experience to construct a traditional kind of argument for the existence of God. When, for instance, I looked at the bush in my backyard I could ask why such a thing of beauty was there. Strictly speaking, it was unnecessary. Its beauty served no pragmatic, utilitarian purpose. The world would survive and continue to evolve without it. In the same way, the world would survive without the plays of Shakespeare, the music of Mozart, the paintings of Renoir or the artistry of Louis Armstrong. And yet we know that our lives would be poorer without them. When the psalmist thanks God for the blessings of creation (Psalm 103), he mentions not only "bread from the earth" but also "wine to gladden men's hearts"; not only the necessities of life (bread), but also those things that "gladden the heart" and make life worth living. So when I asked why this thing of beauty was growing in my backyard, I could only reply that somebody up there wants to delight me, to gladden my heart.

There is a second way to encounter God in such experiences. Rather than drawing back and reflecting on the experience as evidence of the reality of God, I could become so caught up or immersed in the experience that it becomes a direct experience of God. If God is "being itself" (see Chapter 3), then every particular being expresses something of God. And if God is "beauty itself," then in every experience of beauty we discover something of God. In this respect, the visible, tangible world has a "sacramental" function. The natural and human worlds are full of instances of beauty, truth and goodness that make visible the invisible reality of God. As the psalmist puts it, the Lord "fills the earth with his love" (Psalm 32). This is the meaning of the word "sacrament." A sacrament is a visible, tangible sign of a "mystery," an invisible and, in this case, divine reality. Catholics learn as children that the seven sacraments are "outward signs of grace." In the sacraments, the various aspects of God's redemptive love (grace) are made present and real through material elements and ritual. Christ's cleansing and adoptive love is made present and celebrated in the water of baptism; his self-sacrificing and nourishing love in the bread and wine of the Eucharist; his forgiving love in the gestures and words of absolution of the sacrament of reconciliation; his strengthening love in the oil of confirmation, holy orders and the anointing of the sick; his love for and union with the Church in the visible love and union of husband and wife in marriage.

Among Catholics this understanding of the seven sacraments as "channels of grace" did not always translate into an appreciation of the truly sacramental nature of Catholicism. Perhaps this is due to the fact that grace was not understood as the love of God but as some mysterious agent that God dispensed to forgive, heal or strengthen. Or perhaps a puritanical brand of Catholicism made it difficult to find God in those physical, material, worldly realities that otherwise were regarded as threatening "occasions of sin." (Here in Canada we were conveniently provided with both French and English versions of this brand of Catholicism.) Such a puritanical attitude is at odds with what, historically, has been the essential spirit of Catholicism. One of the essential features of the Catholic tradition is its emphasis on the incarnational and sacramental character of the Christian message. If God did not disdain to reveal himself as a flesh-and-blood human being then, by implication, one should not disdain to find God and celebrate his presence in the bodily, tangible, material realities of this world. The God of Christianity, and especially of Catholicism, is found not only in words and in the mind but also in the senses. Thomas Bokenkotter writes: "In Christ the Word became flesh. In the liturgy, the word becomes water, wine, bread and oil. By entering into the material world in the person of Christ, God sanctified all matter and made it an apt vehicle to communicate his spiritual life."[49]

It is for this reason that the Church has consistently rejected any interpretation of the Christian message that would denigrate the body or the material world, or any kind of spirituality that took the form of escape from matter into a world of pure spirit. Whatever else our belief in the "resurrection of the body" means, it affirms the fact that the body as well as the soul is the object of God's saving love. There is a contemporary mindset that prefers an impersonal God or "life force" to the God of Christianity, a God who becomes human flesh and blood and gets his hands dirty by involving himself in human affairs. It prefers esoteric forms of spirituality to "mere religion," which is so open to the corrupting influence of human weakness. It prefers its obsession with angels (pure spirits who get us out of tough situations by their miraculous intervention) to the veneration of the saints (flesh-and-blood human beings who express in a human way the meaning of dying and rising with Christ). Surely this contemporary "spiritual" mentality is, in many of its forms of expression, a new form of puritanism. Whatever impression our Catholic upbringing may have left us with, the Catholic mentality is anything but puritanical. Its attitude to material things, the world, the body, sexuality, etc., is twofold. First, these realities are good in themselves, gifts of God to be enjoyed and celebrated. Second, when used properly, they are realities in which we discover and experience God. In a word, they are "sacramental." An old rhyme sums up this attitude neatly: "Wherever a Catholic sun does shine / There's music and dancing and good red wine / At least I've always found it so / *Benedicamus Domino.*"

---

[49] *Dynamic Catholicism: A Historical Catechism* (New York: Doubleday, 1992), p. 166.

A religious attitude that takes a totally negative view of the pleasures of this world is decidedly not Catholic. Notice that the Church has always balanced times of penance and self-denial with times of feasting and celebration. Indeed, since Vatican II, the word "celebrate" has been revived to describe what is taking place at Mass. The Mass is a celebration of the mystery of redemption. There was a time when only the priest at the altar was referred to as the "celebrant," as if he alone were celebrating. Today, he is more likely to be called the "presider." He presides over a celebration in which the whole community participates. It is true, of course, that some people in the Church feel called to the religious life with its vows of poverty, chastity and obedience. These vows are obviously a renunciation of wealth, sex and power respectively. They do not, however, imply that these things are evil and to be renounced by everyone. The vows of the religious life are intended to remind the rest of us that wealth, sex and power are not ultimate: they are not an end in themselves but a means to becoming fully human and fully Christian.

It is against this background of the incarnational, sacramental nature of Catholicism in general that we should understand the seven sacraments that make up the Church's liturgy. Thirty years ago, those who proclaimed that "God is dead" wanted to obliterate the distinction between the realm of sacred/transcendent reality and the realm of secular/profane reality. There was, we were assured, only one reality – the secular or profane realm. There was no realm of the sacred. Catholic tradition obliterates the distinction between the sacred and the secular in an opposite way – by seeing everything as sacred. This is true in the sense that the visible reality of the allegedly secular world is sacramental; it is a visible sign of the invisible God. The Church has taken some of the elements of this visible world – water, bread, wine, oil – into its worship to serve as pre-eminent signs of God's saving love. As previously noted, each sacrament is a sign and celebration of some aspect of that saving love. If Christ is the "sacrament of God," the visible human being in whom God is revealed, and if the Church is the "sacrament of Christ," the visible continuation of Christ's saving work, then the sacraments are the visible signs of Christ's saving love and redemptive work. As signs, they make that saving love present and effective. Hence we were taught that the sacraments were "effective signs of grace." Bread and wine really become the body and blood of Christ, the words of absolution signify a real forgiveness of sins, etc.

So great was the Catholic emphasis on the effectiveness of the sacramental signs that they were perceived as working automatically (*ex opere operato*). Reminders about the critical role of faith in the reception of the sacraments were not always successful in eliminating this almost magical understanding of the sacraments. The sacraments were seen as having their proper effect as long as they were administered properly. This led to a legalistic preoccupation with the rules for the valid administration of the sacraments. "In an emergency, could one validly baptize with tea or coffee?" was the kind of question we were asked to take seriously. More seriously, boring and uninspiring liturgies were tolerated because they fulfilled the minimum requirements for "validity." About this state of affairs Thomas Bokenkotter makes the following insightful comment: "Preoccupation with the sacraments as causes led to the neglect of their power as symbols."[50] What does Bokenkotter mean by the power of the sacraments "as symbols"? Catholics were taught as children to think of the sacraments as effective *signs* of grace and not as *mere symbols*. And yet it is precisely because the sacraments are "effective signs" that the word "symbol" seems more appropriate, given what we know about the power of symbols. A sign conveys information; it can be translated into words. The walking figure on the traffic light obviously instructs us to "walk." Symbols, however, cannot be so easily translated into words; their message cannot be more adequately expressed than in the symbol itself. A symbol has the power to touch us deeply in an emotional, affective way, to change us and stir us to action. Does this not describe the desired effect of the sacraments? As a Canadian, I may possess a great deal of factual information about my country's history, geography and economy. But I may "know" my country in a much more deeply affective and transforming way by simply looking at the flag or the parliament buildings or hearing the anthem or even by watching some kids play hockey on a frozen pond. Signs inform

---

[50] *Dynamic Catholicism*, p. 179.

us in a rational way; symbols have the power to touch us, motivate us and change us. Whatever theological formula we choose to describe the transforming power of the sacraments, there is an analogy between that power and the transforming power of symbols. A brief reflection on the symbolic power of baptism and the Eucharist may help to clarify the notion that this transformation leads the believer in the direction not only of being fully Christian, but also of being fully human.

*Baptism.* To be baptized, as all Christians know, is to be spiritually reborn and, therefore, to become a child of God. Saying that baptism is an "effective sign" means that through the pouring of or immersion in water and the saying of the words "I baptize you...," the recipient of the sacrament really does become a child of God. The central motif of the ritual of baptism, then, is the theme of rebirth. This is strikingly symbolized in the Easter liturgy. In the Easter vigil service, the liturgy of baptism begins with the priest inviting everyone present to pray for those about to be baptized: "May [God] give them the new life of the Holy Spirit whom we are about to call down on this water." The prayer for the blessing of the baptismal water begins by enunciating the principle that the grace of God is communicated through sacramental signs "which tell us of the wonders of your unseen power." There then follows a recitation of the various ways in which water was seen as symbolic of God's life-giving power in the biblical narrative: the Spirit breathing on the waters in the divine act of creation; the waters of the flood that marked "an end to sin and a new beginning of goodness"; the rescue of the Israelites through the waters of the Red Sea, "an image of God's holy people set free from sin by baptism"; the baptism of Jesus in the waters of the Jordan; the flow of water and blood from the wounded side of the crucified Christ. Notice how all these parallels go beyond the mere requirements for the *valid* administration of the sacrament. They are intended to amplify the symbolic meaning and power of the baptismal ritual and intensify the faith of those receiving the sacrament or renewing their baptismal promises.

The blessing of the baptismal water concludes with the priest lowering the Easter candle – a symbol of Christ – into the baptismal water. The image is that of Christ impregnating, as it were, and making fruitful the font (the "womb" of the Church our mother) so that it might bring forth, through rebirth, children of God. Holding the Easter candle in the water, the priest prays: "May all who are buried with Christ in the death of baptism rise also with him to newness of life." What does the "death of baptism" mean? This idea is more clearly expressed in baptism by immersion, which symbolizes being buried with Christ and rising to a new life with him. Now is this just an example of poetic, metaphorical language to describe religious conversion, or does the experience of rebirth involve an experience of "death" in some real sense? We know that the theme of death and rebirth or resurrection is the central motif of Christianity. In some real sense we are called to die and be reborn; baptism is a symbolic expression of this. Jesus even referred to his coming crucifixion as a baptism: "There is a baptism I must still receive and how great is my distress till it is over" (Luke 12:50). Through our own baptism, then, Christians participate in this "baptism" of Christ; just as Christ rose from the dead, Christians too are reborn.

Looking at all of this from a human, psychological perspective, we can attribute the power of the baptismal symbolism of death and rebirth to the fact that it resonates with and appeals to something deep within us. That something is, according to psychologist Carl Jung, the human desire for rebirth. According to Jung, all religious symbols of rebirth are religious expressions of a universal human desire – the desire for personal, psychological wholeness (see Chapter 1). To be whole or complete, to overcome inner conflict and dividedness, is experienced as death and "rebirth." It is as if one's old self – the incomplete and divided self – has died and a new self has emerged. When people have some kind of radically transforming experience (falling in love, overcoming an addiction, witnessing a tragedy, etc.) their whole way of viewing the world and themselves may be so altered that they resort to this kind of language to describe its effect ("I've been reborn"; "I'm a new man/woman"). We also know that rebirth is not always the result of some sudden, transforming experience. More typically, it is the outcome of slow, gradual, sometimes painful growth. All growth into something new demands the death of the old. All growth is a venture into the unknown and unfamiliar; it demands that I "die" to my old certainties and securities. We have seen, for example, in our discussion of faith that adulthood demands the "death" of one's adolescent self-preoccupation. As Jung puts it, "any growing beyond oneself means death."[51]

The power of the baptismal symbolism of death and rebirth, then, lies partly in the fact that it speaks not only to one's faith but also to one's humanity at a very fundamental level. It is a specifically religious expression of the universal human desire for rebirth or wholeness. As such, it carries a meaning that goes beyond psychological health. It speaks in concrete terms of how rebirth is to be achieved: through faith in the God who is revealed in Jesus Christ. The transformation described in our earlier discussion of the faith experience – the self-transcending and liberating transition from law to grace – can be seen as an experience of rebirth. This reminds us that for baptism to be a truly transforming experience of rebirth, it must be received with faith. What is done for the infant at baptism, therefore, has to be ratified subsequently by an adult act of faith and commitment. This is what the Church asks of its members when they are invited each Easter to renew their baptismal promises.

*The Eucharist.* Catholics believe that at the Last Supper Jesus instructed his followers to commemorate his redemptive death and resurrection in the setting of a shared meal. Catholics also believe that, in this shared meal, they receive, in some real sense, the body and blood of Christ under the appearance of the sacramental elements of bread and wine. The Eucharist or the Mass is, we have been taught, both a sacrifice (making present and visible the sacrifice of Christ) and a meal. It is a representation of both the sacrifice of the cross and the Last Supper, which in turn are the fulfillment of what was prefigured in both the Passover sacrifice and the Passover meal of the Israelites. These two aspects of the Mass should not be separated. The Catholic liturgical renewal since Vatican II has rightly reintroduced the word "celebration" to describe the liturgy of the Mass and indeed all the sacraments. In practice, however, the word is sometimes used in a way that obscures the fact that it is precisely the redemptive sacrifice of Christ that we are

---

[51] *Collected Works*, 5:432.

celebrating. The notion of self-sacrifice or self-offering as a way of participating in the Eucharist used to be a staple of Catholic piety. Catholics were encouraged to identify with Christ's offering of himself made present in the Mass by offering themselves – their life, their work, etc. – to God as part of Christ's self-offering. The Venerable Bede (eighth century) reminds us that, since we share in the priesthood of Christ (we are a "royal priesthood"), we should "offer to God the sacrifice of a holy life."[52]

Now if the meaning of the Eucharist as sacrifice is downplayed, then this notion of participating in the Eucharist through self-sacrifice or self-offering is also overlooked. In doing so, the powerful symbolism of self-sacrifice is lost. Carl Jung wrote a lengthy essay entitled "Transformation Symbolism in the Mass" (Collected Works, 11) in which he explored the psychological symbolism of sacrifice as found in the Mass. Here he reflects on the fact that sacrifice refers to the giving of a gift. Now in ordinary gift-giving it is difficult to be completely altruistic. One's ego inevitably looks for something in return; not necessarily a return gift, but usually some expression of pleasure, gratitude or good will on the part of the recipient. But a sacrifice is different. It is a gift given without any expectation of something in return. For a gift or offering to be truly a sacrifice, then, it is necessary to renounce the claim of one's ego for recompense. This "ego-less" style of offering a sacrificial gift is in keeping with the understanding of the Christian life as rooted in the experience of grace and faith. The Christian life is the believer's total personal response to God's freely given grace or love – a love that cannot be earned or deserved. If, then, the self-offering or sacrifice made at each Mass is to be a renewal of one's Christian faith and commitment, it must be free of any egoistic claim to a reward from God for "being good" or living as God's child. The offering of one's life to God cannot serve the purpose of purchasing from God what has already been given freely. Grace removes the need to attach such an egotistical claim to one's gift and therefore makes a true sacrifice possible.

It is not that Christians do not hope for the reward of eternal life, but the reward has nothing to do with one's so-

---

[52] *Commentary on the First Letter of Peter,* Chapter 2.

called "merits." Eternal life is a gift received in faith. The renewal of one's Christian commitment, in the form of self-offering along with the self-offering of Christ in the Mass, is a true sacrifice if it is free of this egoistic claim that expects God's reward in return for or as recompense for one's good life. Why do we call this claim egoistic? Because it represents the ego's self-asserting and self-seeking desire for certainty, security and control. Such a desire is the antithesis of faith. If I stupidly believe that I can render myself deserving of God's love and the reward of eternal life through my own human efforts, then I create the illusion of certainty and security, of being in control of my own destiny. This in turn means that I must reduce the Christian message to a legalistic kind of religion, to a set of humanly observable rules and regulations. Only in this way can the life I offer to God earn a reward from God. This deadening perversion of the Christian message burdens the life of many a perplexed Catholic. It is clear that Christians are called upon to renounce such an egoistic claim – to renounce this craving for certainty, security and control – and to live by faith. Jesus taught that the Christian commitment involves "losing" oneself (losing one's egoistic desire for security), which paradoxically leads to "finding" oneself. Only self-transcending, self-forgetful commitment leads to true self-possession. Or, as Jung puts it, "If you can give yourself, it proves that you possess yourself."[53]

The fact that the eucharistic sacrifice is celebrated in the setting of a meal stresses the fact that the ultimate purpose of Christ's sacrificial death was to create a community of faith, unity and love. Even on the natural human level the sharing of a meal is symbolic of and a celebration of unity and love. This meaning seems to permeate every kind of sharing of food – from the cake and ice cream at children's birthday parties, to lovers' candlelit dinners, to Super Bowl parties, to family celebrations. Even at funerals the sharing of food expresses unity and solidarity in time of sorrow and loss. And so it is with the eucharistic meal, which expresses the unity and love that should result from a shared faith. But what is the object of that shared faith? It is the love (grace) of God revealed in the sacrificial death and resurrection of Christ. Sacrifice and meal, therefore, cannot be separated since the meal itself is a celebration and renewal of faith in the saving sacrifice.

---

[53] *Collected Works*, 11:390.

Holy communion is an act of participation in the eucharistic meal. The moments after we receive communion are regarded as a time for intensifying our personal, one-on-one relationship with Christ, and so it is. Like any other meal, however, it also represents an intensification of our relationship with all who receive communion and with all Christians. Here again, the aspects of sacrifice and meal come together to emphasize what is important about the life that Christ came to offer his followers.

First, the life of faith must be preceded by a "death." Christ's sacrificial death on the cross made possible his resurrection to a new life. The life of faith – of living "under grace" – is attained by way of the "death" of living under the law. Moreover, as already noted, life in Christ requires the sacrificial "death" or renunciation of all egoistic claims that would make one "deserving" of eternal life. As Bishop Fulton Sheen put it many years ago in one of his famous TV addresses: "If you want to draw a picture of the cross, write a capital 'I' and then cross it out." Sixteen hundred years before Bishop Sheen, St. Ephrem reminded Christians that Christ had to submit to death in order to conquer it: "The Lord was conquered by death and then conquered it in turn. He bowed to death and took it willingly upon him so that he might cast death out against its will."[54] Is this not true of life in general? To live means to grow, and growth is sometimes painful. It is only by "dying" to the old that we can grow into the new. It is only by dying that we live.

Second, it is important to remember that the life of faith is essentially communal. The goal of faith is the freedom from self and self-preoccupation that makes love and community possible. True life is experienced only in communion with others; absolute isolation is, quite literally, "hell." Hence the bread that symbolizes and makes present the sacrificial love of Christ and our own unity and solidarity in Christ is rightly called the "bread of life." The eucharistic sacrifice is symbolic of the "death" of the ego that must precede the experience of that life. The eucharistic meal is symbolic of the fact that life is fully experienced only in communion with others.

---

[54] *On Our Lord*, 3:1.

# 12. WHAT IS ETERNAL LIFE?

All that can be said with certainty about eternal life is that it represents the completion and perfection of the transformation that begins with the experience of grace and faith. On the other hand, those who confess complete ignorance of what constitutes the life of heaven or eternal life or life after death can take comfort in the fact that they are in good company. St. Paul himself declares: "Eye has not seen nor ear heard, nor has it entered into the heart of man, what things God has prepared for those who love him" (1 Corinthians 2:9). The promise of eternal life is an integral part of the Christian message that the Christian accepts in faith. In the person of Christ, the Christian believer sees not only the fulfillment of the Old Testament prophecies, but also a promise for the future. That promise has to do with the ultimate fulfillment of the kingdom of God and the ultimate fulfillment of the individual believer's life in the form of eternal life. The pledge of each believer's victory over death is found in the resurrection of Christ from the dead. If, however, the nature of eternal life is, according to St. Paul, so incomprehensible, what is the point of asking the question "What is eternal life?" I believe that we can discuss the meaning of eternal life because it is not something that begins only after death. It is the continuation, perfection and ultimate fulfillment of one's present life of faith. If this is what eternal life is, then the experience of our present life can give us some insight into the meaning of eternal life.

Most of us were taught as children that eternal life was the life of heaven, which consisted of the experience of seeing God directly (the "beatific vision"). Whatever the theological accuracy of that concept, most of us would have to admit that it is so beyond human comprehension that it does little to stir the imagination or instill a desire for eternal life. Nor was it the image of eternal life favoured by Jesus. When he spoke about eternal life, he did so in parables about the "kingdom of God" or the "kingdom of heaven." If those parables are examined, it seems clear that they do not speak of *individual* reward or fulfillment. There is more to the kingdom of heaven than a group of individuals narcissistically reaping the rewards of their virtuous lives. In Jesus' parables the kingdom of heaven is likened to a vine and its branches, a net cast into the sea that catches good and bad fish, a wedding feast, a banquet, and many other familiar things. What all these images seem to have in common is that they reflect not an individual experience but a social, interpersonal or communal experience. This suggests to me that eternal life is not a reward for individual virtue, but the perfection of our interpersonal and communal life: of the life we live now in communion with others.

Chapter 1 discussed the fact that one of the deepest human and spiritual needs is the need to transcend individual isolation and separation by reaching out to others and forming bonds of love and community. Columnist Rick Salutin, in a *Globe and Mail* article of August 19, 1999, refers to the "stubborn survival of religion" and attributes this in part to the "human desire to be part of something beyond private life." Genuine life is only experienced in communion with others. Jesus says that he came that we might "have life and have it to the full" (John 10:10). Notice that he does not say we will have this life only after death. The life that Jesus promises will indeed reach its fullness and completion only in eternity. But this will be a fulfillment of our present life of faith and love. And what is the essential quality of that life of faith? As already noted, the life of faith is life in communion with others, since the effect of faith is to liberate the individual from self-absorption so that one is able to love others and thereby create community. This experience of love, community and solidarity is the beginning of the life that Jesus promised. Were we not taught as children that the essence of "hell" or eternal death is the pain of separation and isolation? Eternal life, then, must be the opposite – the fullness of oneness and unity, of interpersonal and communal life.

Even in our human secular life this is the case. Complete isolation and separation from others, from the world, from reality is "hell" because it is madness. Life, on the other hand, is what we experience in relation to others and the world. The very word "existence" is derived from the Latin *ex sistere*, to "stand out" towards one's world. Genuine human existence cannot be experienced in isolation. One of the most articulate secular expressions of this understanding of life comes from the work of

Sigmund Freud. Most explanations of Freudian theory are content to speak of Freud's well-known theory of the conflict between the sex instinct and the aggressive, self-preserving "ego instincts." In the final formulation of his theory, however, Freud speaks of deeper and more fundamental conflict that characterizes human life. This is the conflict between the "life instinct" (Eros) and the "death instinct." The death instinct is described as a divisive force. It creates barriers between people through aggression and self-affirmation and on the social level through war, racism, etc. The life instinct, on the other hand, is a unifying force that creates a psychological unity between individuals. The sex or love instinct is just one expression of this deeper drive. According to Freud, the aim of the life instinct is "to combine single human individuals, and after that families, then races, peoples and nations into one great unity, the unity of mankind."[55] The aim of the life instinct is, in other words, the realization of what Christians would call the kingdom of God. Not bad for an "unrepentant atheist," as Freud called himself. (Christians who dismiss Freud because of his atheism seem to be unaware that he grappled with the very question at the heart of the Christian message: Can life triumph over death?)

Many scholars dismiss Freud's theory of the life and death instincts as unscientific speculation. There is no denying that he is not using the term "instinct" in any scientifically accurate way. What he is describing seems to be more like two conflicting sets of attitudes and feelings that give one's life a certain quality or direction or orientation. And is it not true that we all experience within ourselves these two conflicting tendencies? On the one hand, we want to reach out to the world, to form bonds of love and solidarity with others. On the other hand, there is a tendency to withdraw, to live within our own skin, to affirm our independence from the world around us. To some extent we see the world around us as a threat, if not to our safety at least to our individuality. And yet, in the experience of genuine love there is no conflict; we experience both oneness with another or others and, at the same time, a sense of individuality and uniqueness. To the extent that we experience that kind of oneness and unity, we are experiencing that unifying force that Freud calls "life."

---

[55] *Civilization and Its Discontents* (New York: W.W. Norton, 1961), p. 69.

We are also experiencing the beginning of what Christians call "eternal life." Such a life resists death and claims eternity. True love always claims to be "forever."

What relevance does this understanding of life have for the Christian understanding of eternal life? In an essay on "death and hope," the philosopher Gabriel Marcel has reflected on the Christian belief in an afterlife. He observed that most Christians seem to anchor their hope for life after death in the idea of the immortality of the soul. They will survive after death because their immortal soul cannot die. The Christian hope for eternal life, however, is not based on a dubious philosophical conclusion like the immortality of the soul but on God's promise of the resurrection of the body. Marcel finds a particular difficulty with the idea of grounding the hope for immortality in a quality of the individual soul. It then becomes a matter of individual survival and "preoccupation with [individual] survival is still egocentric, whereas a religion worthy of the name finds its centre in God and in God alone."[56] A religion that urges the believer to die to self, to "lose" the self in order to find it, to be self-forgetful in our commitment to others cannot find its hope for eternal life in such an egocentric doctrine.

Marcel suggests that the hope for immortality should not be rooted in some quality of the isolated, individual self, but rather in the bond of love and solidarity that is forged with other human beings. It is not an "object" (the soul) that survives but a bond of love. It is this bond between people that resists death and claims immortality. If that bond is missing, if one is totally isolated, does one even hope for eternal life? Is not despair more likely? It is the death of this bond of love and not the death of the individual self that we find unthinkable. Is the God who commands us to love one another, Marcel asks, capable of ignoring our love or of decreeing its annihilation? "Is it conceivable that a God who offers himself to our love, should range himself *against* this same love, in order to deny it, to bring it to nothingness?"[57] We will indeed experience eternal life as individuals, but as individuals bound together in love and solidarity. That "binding together" that begins in this life constitutes the experience of "life" and the beginning of eternal life.

---

[56] *The Mystery of Being,* Vol. 2 (Chicago: Regnery, 1960), p. 170.

[57] *The Mystery of Being,* Vol. 2, pp. 174-175.

When Jesus promises eternal life, there is no reason to believe that the essential quality of that life is different from that of the life that we are now living. And in our present existence, when do we feel most alive? My answer would be this: in the warmth of friendship, in moments of sexual and/or emotional intimacy, within the family circle, when life is free of discord and enmity or when we feel that we are a vital part of a living community and are making a valuable contribution to the life of that community. I am stressing the fact that life, both temporal and eternal, is an interpersonal experience as opposed to the notion that heaven is an individual experience for those who have "merited" it by their virtuous lives. In the latter view it becomes something individualistic and egocentric. Curiously enough, the saints, whom we think of as enjoying eternal life, seem to have thought very little about "earning" eternal life as a reward for their virtuous lives. They certainly hoped to enjoy eternal life, but only because they were in love with God and with God's children. They expressed that love at times in ways that might strike us as strange or downright silly. (Think of St. Francis preaching to the birds.) On the other hand, who among us has not done silly things when we were in love? That love was the essence of the saints' lives on earth and the basis of their hope for eternal life. It is through these bonds of love and solidarity we forge with others that we begin to experience eternal life. It is love, after all, that makes us feel "alive" and therefore resists death.

This connection between life and love is reflected in the liturgy of the twenty-fifth Sunday in Ordinary Time where we pray: "May we love one another and come to perfection in the eternal life prepared for us." In praying for eternal life, the worshipping community is praying for the ultimate perfection of that love and solidarity that characterizes true interpersonal and communal life. The reader might want to say: This is all very nice as speculation, but what does the Church teach officially about eternal life? Since we are dealing with a mystery, the Church affirms what can be affirmed but allows considerable room for theological reflection. That reflection is what makes up that division of theology called "eschatology." This is sometimes described as the study of the "last things" (death, judgment, heaven and hell). Literally, it refers to the study of the *eschaton*, the last, final, future thing, the ultimate fulfillment of human life and history. What it studies is the object of the believer's hope, which is the full realization of the kingdom of God – that kingdom of love, peace and unity that represents the final victory over death. The Church is an "eschatological community" of faith and hope. Its mission is to reflect in its own life something of the life of that kingdom (as far as that is possible) and to communicate to the world its hope for the full realization of the kingdom of God.

Eschatology has been subjected to a variety of interpretations in the history of Christian thought. For the first Christians, as we know, the *eschaton* represented the end of the world, which they thought was imminent. When these expectations were not fulfilled, the focus shifted from the end of the world to the end of the believer's earthly life. Eschatology became the study of the "last things" – death, judgment, heaven and hell. The "eschatological moment" of transformation, that moment when the old world ends and a new world begins (what the New Testament calls the "new creation"), is now seen as the moment of the believer's death and entry into the eternal life of heaven. This interpretation of eschatology creates a number of problems. First, it reinforces an understanding of the ultimate destiny of the Christian as either reward (heaven) or punishment (hell). Heaven becomes something to be "earned." Second, and precisely because of this legalistic slant, it leaves itself open to an understanding of eternal life in very individualistic and egocentric terms. Finally, it portrays eternal life as something that begins only at the moment of death rather than the perfection and completion of the believer's earthly life of faith.

In the 20th century, some theologians began to interpret eschatology in a way that was more "existential" in the sense that it is more relevant to our present human existence. The moment of a person's "conversion" – the moment when one experiences God's grace and responds with faith – is also seen as an "eschatological" moment. This moment, as we have seen, has a transforming effect since it liberates the believer from the necessity of earning God's love and therefore salvation. Ideally, this in turn transforms one's concern for oneself into concern for others. This transforming experience is an eschatological moment because it inaugurates a whole new way of living, a way of living free of the "baggage" of self-absorption. It empowers people to live with a radically new attitude towards themselves, others and the world. This new attitude is based on the conviction that both the transformed life here and eternal life hereafter are gifts from God and not something to be laboriously fashioned by one's own efforts.

Biblical scholar Robin Scroggs has described this fundamental change of attitude wrought by grace and faith as a "radical perceptual shift" by which "the very roots of a person's thinking, the way the world is looked at, perceived and thus lived in is turned upside down."[58] But the transforming power of grace is never experienced as long as I am completely absorbed in the project of earning my salvation, of trying to put God in my debt so that God "owes" me eternal life. This attitude of self-absorbed anxiety about my own security turns me in on myself rather than opening me up to others. As Scroggs puts it: "Others are useful to me only insofar as they can contribute to my project [of self-justification].... I am not able genuinely to relate to them as an independent person. Thus I cannot be to them a neighbour fulfilling their needs. As long as I strive to justify myself, I cannot love."[59] As long as my number one priority is my own "salvation," what I seemingly do for others is ultimately done for myself. On the other hand, where faith is genuine, the transforming power of grace puts such anxiety about myself to rest and opens me up to others, to the world and its needs. This kind of relatedness to others creates genuine interpersonal and communal life. This is the essential quality of the experience of life, both temporal and eternal. It can be said, then, that eternal life begins here and now in the life of faith.

When thinking about the meaning of eternal life, consider these words of Pope John Paul II: "The definitive form of salvation for man will consist in being completely freed from evil and reaching the fullness of God. This fullness is called, and in fact is, eternal salvation. It is realized in the kingdom of God as an eschatological reality of eternal life."[60] When the pope

---

[58] *Paul for a New Day* (Philadelphia: Fortress Press, 1977), p. 26.

[59] *Paul for a New Day*, p. 9.

[60] *Address in Lisbon,* 1982. See Matthew E. Bunson (ed.), *Papal Wisdom* (New York: Dutton, 1995), pp. 135-136.

speaks of eternal salvation in terms of the complete freedom from evil, I do not believe that he has in mind a state in which each of us individually has become a perfect paragon of what we believe to be virtue. He describes eternal life as the consequence of "salvation," that is, a *healing* of the evil that afflicts human existence. If we understand that evil (or sin) is the state of alienation or separation, then eternal life is the complete healing of that state. It is the complete victory of that unifying force that Freud called the "life instinct." It is the completion and perfection of the love that is a consequence of the life of faith when that faith is genuine. Is it any wonder, then, that faith is the foundation of the Christian life?

When we identify the transforming experience of grace and faith as the "eschatological moment," we mean that through grace and faith one begins to participate, at least in some partial and preliminary way, in the fullness of life that Christ promised. It is the beginning of that "new creation" which the New Testament associates with the realization of the kingdom of God or eternal life. As St. Paul puts it: "For any one who is in Christ, there is a new creation: the old creation has gone, and now the new one is here" (2 Corinthians 5:17). Notice that he does not say that there *will be* a new creation but that there *is* a new creation. God's new creation does not begin only when the present world is destroyed or only after we die and leave this world; it begins here and now whenever we respond with faith to God's love and are thereby sufficiently liberated from ourselves to live, at least in some fragmentary way, the life of God's kingdom.

This understanding of eternal life emphasizes the fact that eternal life begins in this life through the transforming power of grace. In more recent years, the theology of liberation has more fully emphasized the social and communal nature of eternal life. Here the emphasis is on humanity's encounter with God in its striving to liberate itself from social, political and economic oppression. God becomes the God who liberates, who is not so much above us as ahead of us in history and leading us to the fulfillment of that desire for liberation. It is the God we find in the book of Exodus who leads his people to the fulfillment of their destiny.

Eternal life is in this way linked to history. The kingdom of God is seen as the goal and fulfillment of humanity's social, economic and political history. It is the contention of liberation theology that our salvation takes place within the context of our social, political and economic life, not outside of it. Here we have a restatement of the idea that eternal life begins here and now in this present life, but with greater emphasis on this present life as social in character. The freedom from self – from egoism, self-interest and self-preoccupation – that accompanies the experience of grace means that salvation is experienced as freedom – that egoism or sin is the source of all oppression. Consequently, the realization of Christian freedom must include freedom from all those forms of oppression that are the consequences of sin. Salvation and the eternal life it inaugurates must also be experienced as the historical process of liberation from oppression. As the proponents of liberation theology maintain, however, that liberation is part of the process of salvation only when it is liberation *for* communion and human solidarity. Liberation in this sense means liberation from everything that prevents real communion, for that communion is the essence of the life of the kingdom of God. Not only individuals but the human community as such must be transformed to live the life of the kingdom of God.

What, then, can be said about eternal life? It is, like life itself, something experienced in communion with others and it is a life that, where faith is genuine, one begins to experience in at least a partial way in this life. It is not a prize to be won only in eternity. Christian tradition, however, emphasizes a third fact about eternal life. The life that Christ promises must be preceded by death. The gospel of Luke tells us: "As the time drew near for him to be taken up to heaven, Jesus resolutely took the road for Jerusalem" (Luke 9:51). Jesus knew exactly what awaited him in Jerusalem – arrest, torture and crucifixion. Yet he was "resolute" in his determination to endure all of this because he knew that it was only through this suffering and death that he would attain heavenly glorification. Whatever theory of atonement we use to interpret Jesus' suffering and death (see Chapter 10), it represents a pattern to which every Christian must conform in order to attain authentic life. This pattern is that one must die in order to live. In Jesus' own words, we must "lose" our life in order to "find" it. This is consistent with his other paradoxical teachings: we must become poor in order to be rich; we must be last in order to be first; we must become like little children in order to become mature Christians.

Now it goes without saying that one must experience physical death in order to pass into the life of eternity. But what about the preliminary experience of eternal life here on earth? Does that also require that one die in order to live? The fundamental symbol of the Christian faith is the crucifixion and resurrection of Christ, a symbol of death and rebirth. It conveys the idea that to truly live we must first die. And if true or eternal life is life that is experienced in loving communion and solidarity with others, then to experience this life one must die to that deeply rooted egoism that is part of our human condition. It is this egoism that isolates and creates barriers between the self and others and therefore between the self and the true experience of life. That egoism is what Christianity calls "sin." Freud called it the "death instinct." Whatever it is called, it is both a human and religious truth that one must "die" to it in order to truly love and therefore live a life that claims permanence and immortality. Selfishness, aggression, envy, hatred, spitefulness, slander, and domination or control of others are all expressions of that basic egoism. They are not just "sins" for which we will be held accountable. They reflect the condition of sin in which humanity lives and therefore they represent "death" as opposed to life and stand in the way of the human pursuit of the fullness of life. This is a truth well known to both saints and psychotherapists.

The "death" that must precede one's present experience of the life promised by Christ can be understood as part of the effort that the Christian is expected to make in co-operating with the transforming grace of God. Christians are expected to take an active role in their own transformation by their personal efforts to confront and control the egoism that holds them back from the full experience of life. This is the basis for the whole penitential side of Catholic life. Though this aspect has a less obligatory character than it once had, Catholics are still encouraged to perform acts of self-examination and self-discipline – the confession of sins, fasting, acts of penance or self-sacrifice or service to others during Lent, etc. If the understanding of the fundamental Christian message is distorted, then the motives for such practices will be distorted. These are not things to be done grudgingly in the hope of a reward in the next life. What kind of God would reward us for making ourselves miserable? Self-sacrifice is rather something done willingly in order to overcome the egoism that holds us back from being fully alive. Neither God nor life itself rewards us for being masochists.

# PART V
# THE CHRISTIAN PARADOX

There is more to the Christian life than belonging to a Church and living by a set of moral rules. The call to faith is a call to conversion. If I "convert" some Canadian dollars into U.S. dollars or English pounds, I am exchanging one type of currency for another. Christian conversion is something like that. It is a change of heart in which one set of values – the currency by which our world all too often lives – is exchanged for a radically different set of values. Jesus challenged his followers to find themselves by losing themselves, to find a different kind of wealth by being poor, to discover wisdom in simplicity and greatness in humility and, finally, to die in order to live. Our task in this final section is to understand these paradoxical values as being valid in human and psychological as well as religious terms. From both the religious and the human point of view we can ask:

1) What kind of richness is found in poverty?

2) What kind of wisdom is found in simplicity?

3) What kind of greatness is found in humility?

# 13. WHY ARE THE POOR RICH?

Travel writer Bill Bryson[61] concluded from his sojourn in England that the happiness of the British is due in part to the fact that they are easy to please and "like their pleasures small." They are, he observes, "the only people in the world who think of jam and currants as thrilling constituents of a pudding or cake." For Americans, on the other hand, "gratification, instant and lavish, is a birthright." There may be some tongue-in-cheek hyperbole in Bryson's choice of words, but he leaves no doubt about the effect on his own outlook of this British attitude that, when it comes to pleasure, less is more. "Gradually," he writes, "I came round to their way of thinking and my life has never been happier…. Before long I came to regard all kinds of activities – asking for more toast in a hotel, buying wool-rich socks at Marks & Spencer, getting two pairs of trousers when I only really needed one – as something daring, very nearly illicit. My life became immensely richer."

Bryson does not elaborate, so we can only surmise in what sense his life became "richer" by doing with less. It is clear from his words, however, that "richer," in this instance, means "happier." Bryson's experience is, of course, a common human experience in which one learns that material possessions represent only one kind of wealth and not the most enriching kind either. The fact that some things are more important to our happiness than material possessions is a truth one comes to appreciate in the process of becoming human. Everyone then is challenged by this question: What kind of enrichment do I want? What kind of wealth is more important to me than material wealth?

This, I believe, is the challenge implied in the words with which Jesus begins his "Sermon on the Mount": "Happy are the poor in spirit; theirs is the kingdom of heaven" (Matthew 5:3). Biblical scholars maintain that this was not a single sermon delivered on a single occasion but a collection of Jesus' teachings given over the course of his public ministry. Nevertheless it

---

[61] *Notes from a Small Island* (Toronto: McClelland and Stewart, 1995), pp. 72-74.

reads like a sermon because it is possible to find a unifying theme. In general it deals with the kind of spirit, attitude or motivation that should inform the life of the Christian: of anyone who wants to participate in the life of the kingdom of God and respond to the "good news" of that kingdom that Jesus had begun to announce. In short, the Sermon on the Mount (Matthew 5–7) describes the Christian personality, the qualities that should characterize the life of the person of genuine faith. To be a Christian means to be poor in spirit, pure of heart, the salt of the earth, the light of the world; one whose virtue goes deeper than the legalism of the Pharisees and does not seek human recognition or reward; who puts concern for the kingdom of God ahead of material concerns; who is humble, non-judgmental, constant in prayer, etc.

I find it significant that this long discourse on Christian values, attitudes and lifestyle should begin with what we refer to as the eight "beatitudes." In more recent translations of the Bible the word "blessed," which used to introduce each beatitude, has been replaced by the word "happy" ("happy" are the poor in spirit, the gentle, the pure of heart, etc.). This perhaps conveys more clearly the meaning of the word "blessed" and the idea that happiness is to be found in the practice of the beatitudes. But this does not refer exclusively to happiness in some eternal afterlife. Jesus proclaims that *in this present life* it is paradoxically the meek, the sorrowful, the oppressed, etc. – those whom the world often considers "losers" – who have found a more genuine kind of happiness. It is clear that, even in purely human terms, it is sometimes preferable to be a "loser" than a "winner," such as when one's moral integrity is at stake. I believe it was Will Rogers who said, "I would rather be the man who bought the Brooklyn Bridge than the man who sold it."

It is interesting that the Sermon on the Mount should begin with a call to "poverty of spirit." Would it therefore be fair to suggest that the call to be poor (in whatever sense Jesus meant it) is so fundamental that its absence or neglect makes it impossible to respond to the Christian message? Jesus himself claims that there is a way of being "rich" that makes entering the kingdom of heaven as difficult as it would be for a camel to pass through the eye of a needle (Matthew 19:23-24). Poverty of spirit is seen as being in some sense a prerequisite for happiness

– not only in eternity but even for one's present earthly life. St. Alphonsus Liguori emphasizes that it is one's *present* happiness that is in question: "To the poor in spirit the Kingdom of Heaven is assigned as a present recompense, for theirs *is* the Kingdom of Heaven."[62]

Poverty, then, is in some sense a fundamental ingredient of the Christian life and a prerequisite for happiness in our present life. In other words it is, rightly understood, both a religious and a human value. Before attempting to understand in what sense that is true, perhaps it is important to remember an important fact about the nature of happiness: it is something not entirely within our control. Happiness is something received, not manufactured; something that "happens" to us, not something achieved. It is paradoxical in that the more we consciously pursue it, the more it eludes us. We cannot manufacture our own happiness in a self-absorbed way. Happiness is ours when we commit ourselves in a self-forgetful way to what is beyond or transcends ourselves: a task to be accomplished, people to love, an ideal to pursue, a cause or a God to serve, etc. Perhaps then we should not completely discard the old translation – *Blessed* are the poor in spirit – since the word "blessed" conveys the idea that happiness is a blessing rather than a personal accomplishment.

The teachings of Jesus are, in many instances, a reflection of this fundamental paradox. They counsel the Christian not to try to find happiness in those things the world associates with happiness – wealth, power, popularity, etc. Accordingly, we must lose our life in order to find it (Matthew 10:39); we must become as little children in order to achieve greatness (Matthew 18:4); we must be last in order to be first (Matthew 20:16); we must become the servant of all in order to exercise real authority (Matthew 20:20); we must become poor in order to possess what is truly worth possessing (Matthew 5:3). And ultimately – for this is the meaning of the fundamental Christian symbol – we must die in order to live. This is the meaning of the cross and the fundamental paradox that Jesus' life reveals. The truth that Jesus proclaimed and that is intended

---

[62] Quoted in Jill Haak Adels, *The Wisdom of the Saints* (New York: Oxford University Press, 1987), p. 127.

to "make us free" is a paradoxical one. It is a truth that turns human thinking upside down. Consequently, it is a truth that may prove to be to our human way of thinking an "obstacle" or "madness," to use St. Paul's words, when we are told that what we consider weakness is really power, what we consider foolishness is really wisdom, what we consider poverty is really wealth and what we consider death is really life. St. Paul believed that the paradoxical message of Christ's cross could not be explained philosophically. Only through faith is it possible to affirm that "God's foolishness is wiser than human wisdom and God's weakness is stronger than human strength" (1 Corinthians 17:25).

The point of the first beatitude is that what we consider wealth is really poverty and what we consider poverty is really wealth. Seen in this light, the poverty that Jesus advises is not simply deprivation for its own sake; it is deprivation for the sake of a more rewarding kind of wealth or exchanging one kind of wealth for another. This kind of poverty has a positive value and Jesus not only preaches it but incarnates it in his own person. If the incarnation was intended to show us how God would live if he were a human being, then Jesus' choice to be poor was an integral part of that revelation. St. Bernard of Clairvaux put it this way: "Poverty was not found in heaven. It abounded on earth but man did not know its value. The Son of God, therefore, treasured it and came down from heaven to choose it for Himself, to make it precious to us."[63] If our faith were simple enough, we might simply imitate Jesus' poverty and discover through experience the truth about poverty that he wanted to convey. That truth is not that if we choose to be poor we will be miserable but virtuous (real virtue is not miserable) and therefore deserving of an eternal reward. It is rather that the choice of poverty in some way makes one more fully human and therefore on the way to a more genuine happiness.

Saints are venerated because they are living embodiments of various aspects of the Christian life. In popular Christian imagination no saint exemplifies the attitude that finds positive value and happiness in voluntary poverty more than St. Francis of Assisi does. Perhaps this is so because his embracing

---

[63] *The Wisdom of the Saints*, p. 126.

of poverty was so absolute and undertaken with such dramatic and even romantic flair. Appearing before the bishop of Assisi with his well-off father, who was disinheriting him because of his apparent insanity, Francis stripped himself of even the clothes he was wearing and returned them to his father. The bishop, so the story goes, clothed Francis in a rough brown tunic belonging to his gardener. This was the origin of the Franciscan habit. From that point on Francis did not merely endure poverty stoically; he began a life-long love affair with what he called "Lady Poverty." "If we embrace Holy Poverty very closely," he said, "the world will come to us and will feed us abundantly."[64] In reflecting on the meaning of poverty of spirit our task is to understand this paradox. In what sense does the world "feed" those who are poor in spirit? In what way does poverty enrich us?

In trying to answer these questions, we must remember that Jesus' contention that it is the poor who are truly rich is not just a religious truth to be accepted on faith. It is also a philosophical and psychological truth concerning human nature and the human condition. Perhaps the most explicit psychological statement of the truth of this paradox is to be found in the work of psychoanalyst Erich Fromm (1900–1980). In his distinction between the "having" and "being" modes of existence, I believe that Fromm echoes the teaching of Jesus on poverty of spirit. Though he rejected his Orthodox Jewish faith at age 26, Fromm retained the deeply rooted humanism of the Jewish tradition. The result was a humanistic type of psychoanalysis that differed fundamentally from Freudian psychoanalysis. People fell ill and were in need of therapy, Fromm argued, not so much because of a conflict of instinctual drives (sex and aggression) but because modern society tended to alienate its members from themselves, from others and from nature. To be alienated or estranged from oneself means simply that instead of living in accord with one's own human nature one lives in accordance with the dominant values, ideas, tastes, lifestyle, opinions, ideologies, etc., of one's culture or society. In a word, we *conform*. For society to function some degree of conformity is necessary. However, when such conformity

---

[64] *The Wisdom of the Saints*, p. 127.

reaches the point where one's deepest feelings and convictions are repressed for the sake of being accepted, popular or politically correct, then one begins to lose touch with one's true self and presents a pseudo-self to the world. One has then developed what Fromm calls "social character" – the character traits necessary to live and prosper in a given society. The price of such conformity is self-alienation – separation from our true self – in which we no longer feel that we are the authors of our own thoughts or the subject of our own feelings and actions.

Alienation happens, in other words, when our social character replaces and represses our essential humanity. Thus it may happen that a person's true self, with all its potentialities, is never actualized. As Fromm puts it, "The whole life of the individual is nothing but the process of giving birth to himself; indeed, we should be fully born when we die – although it is the tragic fate of most individuals to die before they are born."[65] With these words Fromm reminds us that, from a human perspective, death is a tragic event for even the most long-lived and productive people, since it leaves us with a sense of "unfinished business" – if only the business of giving birth to our true selves and our full human potential. This sense of incompleteness, of not being fully ourselves, of being alienated from our true self, is also part of the tragic dimension of life. It occurs when we feel that we are not being true to our own deepest feelings and convictions. This lack of integrity is seen by Fromm as a source of shame: "The inability to act spontaneously, to express what one genuinely feels and thinks, and the resulting necessity to present a pseudo self to others and oneself, are the root of the feeling of inferiority and weakness. Whether or not we are aware of it, there is nothing of which we are more ashamed than of not being ourselves, and there is nothing that gives us greater pride and happiness than to think, to feel and to say what is ours."[66]

This kind of self-possession is what Fromm calls the "being" mode of existence. I believe it is relevant to what Jesus has to say about being "poor in spirit" because he contrasts it

---

[65] *The Sane Society* (Greenwich, CT: Fawcett Publications, 1965), p. 32.

[66] *Escape from Freedom* (New York: Avon Books, 1965), p. 288.

with the "having" mode of existence. This is seen as our fundamental choice – to be or to have. These choices represent two fundamentally opposed approaches to life or two fundamentally different types of *ethical* character structure. Fromm believes that the call to renounce "having" (possessions, power, etc.) in order to *be*, to ground my identity in what I am (the subject of my human powers) and not in what I possess, is at the heart of the ethical teachings of both the Old and New Testaments. From this perspective, the real danger of wealth or possessions is not the mere fact of having but the loss of self that results from finding my identity and self-worth in what I have rather than what I am. As Fromm remarks: "If I am what I have and if what I have is lost, who then am I"?[67] This question recalls the words of Jesus: "What gain, then, is it for a man to have won the whole world and to have lost or ruined his very self?" (Luke 9:25). The hazard of possessions is the loss of self.

Fromm's distinction between having and being derives from his critique of modern consumer society. (The trend towards consumerism has certainly not been reversed since his death in 1980.) The psychological residue of consumerism is the having mode of existence. If I am identified with what I possess, it is difficult to experience myself as the active subject of my thoughts, feelings and actions. I am alienated from my personal experiences because the having mode turns those experiences into possessions. Fromm's examples of language patterns as symptoms of this kind of self-alienation are perhaps overstated but are nonetheless illustrative. In everyday speech, he points out, nouns increasingly replace verbs. Thus, "I *have* a problem" replaces "I *am* troubled"; I *have* insomnia" replaces "I *cannot* sleep"; "I *have* a good marriage" replaces "I *am* happily married." This trend, which Fromm noticed 25 years ago, is still alive and well. Today, couples who love one another "*have* a good relationship" and someone who is annoyed with something "*has* a problem" with it. Let's just say that Fromm "had a problem" with this kind of speech pattern because he believed it was symptomatic of "a hidden, unconscious alienation" in which feelings are transformed into possessions. When I hear a youngster who is shy described as "*having* social

---

[67] *To Have or to Be?* (New York: Harper & Row, 1976), 109.

anxiety syndrome," I am inclined to think that Fromm has a point.

Recalling the concept of "social character," Fromm suggests that in the modern consumer society, where the having mode is dominant, the formula for a sense of personal identity is: *I am = what I have and what I consume.* One's possessions become one's identity. The self-alienating effect of this requires little explanation. As long as it dominates one's life it blocks the development of the being mode of existence. In the being mode, the emphasis is not on having or possessing but on *acting.* Acting, in this context, does not refer to outward activity or "busyness"; it refers to a kind of inner activity that Fromm describes as the productive use of our human powers of reason and love. This presupposes the freedom to express thoughts and feelings that are genuinely my own. It is clear that if I overidentify myself with my possessions or with some dominant collective mentality, I am not free to be myself. I no longer experience myself as the active subject of my thoughts, feelings and actions.

The essence of the being mode of existence is the freedom to be myself. It is the freedom to think my own thoughts, speak my own words, experience my own emotions and thereby give expression to my own human powers of reason and love. What makes this way of being "productive" (to use Fromm's term) is the fact that those human powers grow and develop with practice. The more we think for ourselves, the greater our powers of critical reason become. The more we love, the greater our capacity for love. The more we express our truest feelings, the greater our freedom of self-expression becomes. On the other hand, what we merely possess is diminished by use. Fromm, therefore, concludes: "What is spent is not lost, but what is kept is lost."[68] In the story of the "burning bush" that burns but is not consumed (Exodus 3), he finds a biblical symbol of this paradox. At the profoundly human level, one is enriched not by hoarding but by "spending" or exercising one's human powers of reason and love. In this respect, they are unlike material possessions, which are diminished or devalued by use – a truth brought home to us the minute we drive that new car off the dealer's lot. The ability to think thoughts,

---

[68] *To Have or to Be?,* p. 110.

experience feelings and act on convictions that are truly my own grows with practice and allows me to discover my identity as the subject of such truly human activity.

Now I believe that Jesus expressed a similar truth in the following words: "For anyone who has will be given more, and he will have more than enough; but from anyone who has not, even what he has will be taken away" (Matthew 13:12). In Mark's account, these words are preceded by the words "The amount that you measure out is the amount you will be given – and more besides" (Mark 4:24-25), which clearly echoes Fromm's statement that "what is spent is not lost." It is also interesting that in Matthew's gospel these words are repeated as a conclusion to the parable of the talents (Matthew 25:29). Perhaps then we could attempt this paraphrase of Jesus' words: Those who are rich in those things that can be spent or used in a humanly productive way – knowledge, love, compassion, generosity, etc. – will find that these attributes will grow with use. They "will be given more and will have more than enough." Those, on the other hand, who are lacking in these personal qualities ("anyone who has not") and who find their identity and security in material possessions will find their possessions diminishing with use and therefore a source of anxiety. At the same time, they will find their sense of self-worth, identity and security to be diminished and devalued since they have identified themselves with what they possess. In other words, if all you "have" is what you possess you are impoverished. The truly rich are the "spendthrifts" who experience human and spiritual growth through giving of themselves.

These words of Jesus turn the popular understanding of the "haves" and "have nots" upside down. So also does Fromm's distinction between being and having. Those who truly "have" are those who are rich in the human capacity for reason, love, compassion, etc. Those who "have not" are those who possess to the point of identifying themselves with their possessions. For these, the loss of possessions amounts to the loss of self – surely the most tragic kind of poverty. The fifth-century bishop St. Peter Chrysologus applied this paradox to the practice of giving to the poor: "What you give away in mercy will enrich you. Do not lose then what you have by clinging to it, but gather up by giving away. In giving to the poor you give to yourself, and what you do not give away you will not have."[69]

Jesus' words about poverty, then, have a humanistic as well as a religious value, if indeed it is appropriate to separate the two. To renounce possessions and control is both a religious and a human value since it liberates a person to "be" the active subject of his own human powers. To be liberated from possessions is to be liberated from the tyranny they exercise when we invest our identity and security in them. And yet renouncing our possessions does not mean simply that we are to do without material possessions. For the average person this would be impossible.

Jesus spells out the attitude he expects his followers to have towards money and possessions:

"No one can be a slave of two masters; he will either hate the first and love the second, or treat the first with respect and the second with scorn. You cannot be the slave of both God and money.

"That is why I am telling you not to worry about your life and what you are to eat, nor about your body and how you are to clothe it. Surely life means more than food and the body more than clothing! Look at the birds in the sky. They do not sow or reap or gather into barns; yet your heavenly Father feeds them. Are you not worth much more than they are? Can any of you, for all his worrying, add one single cubit to his span of life? And why worry about clothing? Think of the flowers growing in the fields; they never have to work or spin, yet I assure you that not even Solomon in all his regalia was robed like one of these. Now if that is how God clothes the grass in the field which is there today and thrown into the furnace tomorrow, will he not much more look after

---
[69] Sermon 43.

169

you, you men of little faith? So do not worry; do not say, 'What are we to eat? What are we to drink? How are we to be clothed?' It is the pagans who set their hearts on all of these things. Your heavenly Father knows you need them all. Set your hearts on his kingdom first, and on his righteousness, and all these other things will be given you as well." (Matthew 6:24-33)

It would be a mistake, I believe, to interpret these words of Jesus as counselling us to adopt an attitude of indifference towards our physical and material needs. Food, clothing and shelter are necessities; Jesus assures us that "your heavenly Father knows that you *need* them all." What is condemned is enslaving ourselves to material possessions ("You cannot be the slave both of God and money"). That enslavement takes place when, according to Jesus, we make things like food, clothing and shelter the object of "worry."

Herein lies a problem for most people, for a lifetime free of worry about such things seems like an impossible dream. Perhaps Jesus' words lose something in translation. Whatever the linguistic merits of the translation of Jesus' words as "Do not worry" may be, I believe the translators of more recent versions of the New Testament have done us a disservice by abandoning the wording of the older translations – "Be not *anxious*." Perhaps Jesus' hearers were not sensitive to the distinction between worry and anxiety, but today's readers of the New Testament are, at least realizing that it is impossible not to "worry" about material needs that Jesus himself recognized as necessities. "Do not worry" seems like cruel advice to give to someone who is unemployed, or to a single mother on welfare, or to a victim of corporate "downsizing." I doubt that Jesus would say "Don't worry, be happy" to such people. "Be not anxious," however, means something quite different. Worry is about external problems; anxiety is about oneself. It is almost impossible not to worry about the spectre of unemployment or the mortgage that has to be paid off or the cost of educating one's children. But these are problems external to oneself and do not normally reflect negatively on the person who has to deal with them. If I am struggling with financial setbacks or poor economic prospects, it does not necessarily mean that I have failed as a human being. If I allow myself to feel like a failure, then worrying about external problems becomes anxiety about myself and about my worth as a person. While it is difficult not to worry about material needs – food, clothing, shelter – it is a mistake, according to Jesus, to be *anxious* about such things. It is wrong – both religiously and psychologically – to let such concerns affect one's self-esteem or become a source of anxiety about one's self-worth. The Christian's self-esteem is rooted ultimately in the love of God who "knows that we need all these things."

Here again, I believe, the Christian attitude towards material possessions – or the lack thereof – converges with what Fromm would call the "being mode of existence." In the being mode, I identify myself with and experience myself as the subject of my own thoughts and feelings, the speaker of my own words, the author of my own responsible decisions and the seeker of the meaning of my own existence. Material possessions are simply there to make all this "inner" activity possible. If, on the other hand, I identify myself with those possessions, I can become alienated from my true self, from what makes me truly human. This is what Fromm calls the "having" mode of existence. If my identity and self-esteem are rooted in what I possess – house, car, savings, investments, etc. – and if my identity and self-worth fluctuate with the size and quality of those possessions, then I have become alienated from myself. I have become, to use St. James' image, "like someone who looks quickly at himself in a mirror and then walks away and forgets what he looks like" (James 1:24). The having mode of existence causes people to forget who they really are, to forget what makes them truly human. In the same vein, Jesus tells his followers not to find their identity, security and self-worth in their possessions. If one's self-esteem is rooted in God's abiding and unconditional love for us – in "the kingdom of God and his righteousness" – then the admittedly worrisome economic vicissitudes of life will not become a source of anxiety about oneself.

We are led to the conclusion that the "poverty of spirit" expected of the Christian has more to do with an *attitude* towards material possessions than with the possessions themselves. As St. Augustine put it, "A man's poverty before God is judged by the disposition of his heart, not by his coffers."[70] What is to be said, then, about those saints of old who took the call to poverty with almost alarming literalness? The legends of the saints tell stories of desert fathers, monks and hermits who lived lives of extreme deprivation in terms of food, clothing, shelter and creature comforts. Nor is this near obsession with poverty confined to austere, "other-worldly" saints. The very human and beloved Don Bosco is reported to have said as he was dying, "Take my pocketbook and purse out of my soutane and, if there is any money in them, send them to Don Rua. I want to die so poor that they may say that Don Bosco died without leaving a halfpenny."[71] For those who practised it, this kind of poverty was a way of making possible a complete and total dedication to "the kingdom of God and his righteousness." If they are venerated rather than dismissed as eccentrics, it is because their lives are reminders that "having" is not the supreme value in life; that the higher values of truth, justice, compassion and one's own humanity are not to be sacrificed to the need to possess and control.

Nor does one need to be religiously motivated to appreciate this truth. The current, purely secular movement towards voluntary poverty or the simplifying of life recognizes the dehumanizing effect of preoccupation with the "stuff" that clutters up our lives. A recent newspaper article[72] describes "voluntary simplicity," the trend towards abandoning high paid but high pressure jobs in order "to get back in touch with what is *really* important – family, health and happiness," as "the first great trend of the new millennium." Couples who have followed this trend describe the benefits they have enjoyed: "We see our kids and we don't work insane hours." "You can leave behind a lot of stresses. And a lot of possessions that clutter up your life. You get out of the trap of trying to impress everybody."

Since the move towards voluntary simplicity usually involves giving up material wealth, it requires something of a leap of faith. And it is precisely in the context of faith that the

---

[70] *The Wisdom of the Saints,* p. 127.

[71] *The Wisdom of the Saints,* p. 128.

[72] "Broke, not broken," *The Globe and Mail,* April 15, 2000.

Christian teaching on wealth and possessions is to be understood. Christian faith is a call to find security not in the tangible, visible world of things, but in what is invisible and beyond control, that is, in the grace and promise of God. In the words of biblical scholar Rudolf Bultmann, faith involves "accepting completely different standards as to what is to be called death and what [is to be called] life. It means accepting the life that Jesus gives and is – a life that, to the world's point of view, cannot be proved to exist."[73] Now "the life that Jesus gives," reduced to its simplest terms, is the life of a child of God. Not only are we unable to prove our status as children of God in any human way, we are also unable to earn it or be deserving of it by any human effort. Notice the fact that Bultmann stresses that faith means "accepting" this life as a gift. Faith means accepting God's gift and believing in God's desire to be a father to us. That gift (grace) and the response of faith become the ultimate source of the believer's identity and security.

Trying to find that identity and security in any human possession or accomplishment becomes an obstacle to faith. To do so is to hand over a certain control over one's life to those things in which one tries to find security. It is to become, as it were, enslaved to them or dependent on them. What could have been enjoyed as part of God's creation now becomes – through a human decision – God's rival ("this world") and a human burden (as those who have opted for "voluntary simplicity" have discovered). When security is sought in material possessions, those possessions become the rival and enemy of something more important, whether it be God ("You cannot be the slave both of God and money") or family or health or happiness.

It is in this way – through the human decision to find security in human achievements, creations or possessions – that one becomes enslaved to the "visible and tangible sphere." As Bultmann puts it, "Since the visible and tangible sphere is essentially transitory, the man who bases his life on it becomes the prisoner and slave of corruption."[74] It should be clear that Bultmann is not claiming that the material world or material

---

[73] *Theology of the New Testament,* Vol. 2 (New York: Scribners, 1955), p. 75.

[74] "The New Testament and Mythology" in *Kerygma and Myth: A Theological Debate* (New York: Harper Torchbook, 1961), p. 19.

possessions are evil in themselves. They become obstacles to faith only when one's attitude to them constitutes what St. Paul called "living after the flesh," succumbing to the all-too-human tendency to find security in concrete and visible possessions and achievements. When one's identity and security are found in what is possessed, then those things that were meant to be enjoyed begin to exercise power and control the owner. No wonder Jesus warned his followers not to be "anxious" about material possessions. A certain amount of financial security is desirable, but when financial security becomes our ultimate source of security and identity, we become prey to the kind of anxiety that deprives us of true enjoyment of our possessions.

Perhaps this is what St. Francis meant when he said that poverty enriches us. The poverty of which he speaks is rooted in faith that, according to Bultmann, means "to abandon all merely human security and thus to overcome the despair which arises from the attempt to find security, an attempt which is always in vain."[75] By liberating us from the anxiety that results from rooting our security in material possessions, poverty of spirit enriches us by allowing us to enjoy what we possess. This requires a certain "detachment" on our part. This detachment is experienced when ultimate security is found in God rather than in what God has created. This makes possible the enjoyment of that creation as a gift. The teaching of the Second Vatican Council puts it this way: "Redeemed by Christ and made a new creature in the Holy Spirit, man is able to love the things themselves created by God *and ought to do so*. He can receive them from God and respect and reverence them as flowing constantly from the hand of God. Grateful to his Benefactor for these creatures, *using and enjoying them in detachment and liberty of spirit*, man is led forward into a true possession of the world, as having nothing, yet possessing all things."[76] To "have" nothing (in the sense in which Fromm uses the word) makes it possible to enjoy everything.

Owning one's dream home or a luxury car or the very latest in computer technology or electronic gadgetry may prove

---

[75] *Jesus Christ and Mythology* (London: S.C.M. Press, 1960), p. 40.

[76] *Pastoral Constitution on the Church in the Modern World*, #37. [Italics mine.]

to be less fun than anticipated when those possessions are forced to do more than they were intended to do: give the owner a sense of self. When, on the other hand, the sense of identity and self-worth is rooted in something else, those possessions have a way of becoming less important or even unnecessary. And what is unimportant – unrelated to one's sense of self – is no longer a source of anxiety.

## 14. WHY ARE THE SIMPLE WISE?

It is frequently the case that Jesus' call to be "pure in heart" in order that we might "see God" is translated into a simple equation: If I am pure and good in this life, I will be blessed with the vision of God in eternity. Unfortunately, this equation is frequently understood in a way that severely restricts the meaning of both "pure" and "seeing God." It relegates the vision of God to a reward in the afterlife. But is there a sense in which we can "see God" in this life? The meaning of Jesus' words is further obscured when the meaning of purity is restricted to a puritanical ideal of sexual propriety. But one may be "pure" in this sexual sense and, at the same time, have a heart full of envy, malice, pride, bigotry, self-righteousness and hostility. Such a heart cannot see God since it is so self-absorbed that it sees little beyond its own self-interest. St. John Vianney once remarked: "The eyes of the world see no farther than this life, as mine see no farther than this wall when the Church door is shut. The eyes of the Christian see deep into eternity."[77] Two questions come to mind: (1) What does "seeing into eternity" mean? (2) What enables the Christian to do this?

The obvious answer to our second question is "faith." Faith enables us to see God or to see into eternity. St. Thomas, the doubting apostle, refused to believe the reality of the risen Christ unless he could see and touch the wounds of the one who had been crucified. When he saw them, he did not say, "Yes, it is Jesus," but uttered the more profound profession of faith, "My Lord and my God!" Commenting on this scene, Pope St. Gregory the Great remarks: "Faith is the proof of what cannot be seen. What is seen gives knowledge, not faith. When Thomas saw and touched, why was he told, 'You have believed because you have seen me'? Because what he saw and what he believed were different things. God cannot be seen by mortal man."[78] In the context of religious faith, the expression "seeing is believing" is not quite true. Seeing (knowledge) and believing (faith) are not the same thing. Seeing, as St. Gregory points out, leads only to knowledge. And yet, as the apostle Thomas discovered, what

---

[77] Quoted in Jill Haak Adels, *The Wisdom of the Saints*, p. 29.

[78] *The Wisdom of the Saints*, p. 177.

is seen can lead to faith in what is not seen. "What he saw and what he believed were different things." Thomas did not see God directly ("God cannot be seen by mortal man"). He saw the human, wounded Jesus, but by faith he saw in him his "Lord and God." Perhaps, then, there is a reciprocal relationship between seeing and believing. Seeing leads one to faith, but what we believe is more than what we see. By faith we "see deep into eternity."

Jesus advised his followers that their happiness was linked to this kind of vision, the precondition of which was a certain kind of purity. "Happy the pure in heart: they shall see God" (Matthew 5:8). But what did he mean by purity of heart? The most obvious meaning of purity in a moral sense is freedom from sin. The beatitude that calls the Christian to purity of heart is a reminder that sin is found not just in external conduct but also – and more essentially – in the dispositions of the heart. Further along in the Sermon on the Mount (Matthew 6:20-30), Jesus elaborates on this idea with two examples: murder and adultery. The evil of murder is not just in the external act but in the anger and hatred that motivate the act. Likewise, the evil of adultery is not just in the act itself but in the lustful desire that motivates it. One is reminded of former American president Jimmy Carter's admission that he had been guilty of committing adultery "in his heart." Given the use that the media tend to make of such gossipy items, President Carter's admission may have been ill-advised. Nevertheless, it is in stark contrast to a later president's convoluted attempts to prove that his actual extra-marital dalliance was not technically adultery. Moral purity, Jesus states, is purity in one's heart and not just in one's external conduct.

These words of Christ concerning purity of heart imply that one's heart must be purified of sin if one is to be able to see God. St. Theophilus of Antioch (second century) suggests that God is seen with the "eyes of the mind" just as the physical world is seen with our bodily eyes. And just as we cannot see the physical world if our eyes are blinded by disease or injury, "So too your mind has eyes, but these can be blinded by your sins and evil actions.... If a man is a sinner, he cannot see God.... If you understand this and if you live in purity and holiness and uprightness you can see God."[79] Now Theophilus was speaking of purity of heart as enabling one to see God in an eternal afterlife ("Once you have put aside your corruptible self and put on the incorruptible, you will see God"). But is there a sense in which sin or a lack of purity of heart can prevent us from seeing God in this life? It is clear that one can speak of seeing God in this life only in a qualified sense. Christians believe that the direct vision of God belongs not to this present life but to the life of eternity. If by faith, then, the Christian is able to "see into eternity," this would refer to an indirect vision of God – to see, for instance, God in the beauty of his creation or to see his presence in one's fellow human beings or in the circumstances of one's life.

Surely these instances of "seeing" God require the same purity of heart as seeing God directly in eternity. And yet, why do some find God, or at least the reality represented by that name, in creation and others do not? Why do some see God in their life experience and others do not? Because to see simply with one's bodily eyes is not sufficient. To be aware of the deeper implications of what one sees – to see the eternal in the temporal – one must see with the "heart." St. Augustine puts it this way: "How foolish, then, are those who try to find God through the use of their bodily eyes! It is through the heart that God is seen…. And just as the light that surrounds us cannot be seen except through eyes that are clear, so neither is God seen unless that through which He can be seen is pure."[80] In one of his sermons, Augustine gives this hint about what such purity of heart might mean: "One must look into the human heart, to see in what direction it is turned and on what point its gaze is fixed."[81] These words suggest to me that purity of heart is a matter of what one values and, therefore, what one's intentions and goals are. Purity of heart, in other words, refers to the purity of one's intentions.

Much of Jesus' Sermon on the Mount is concerned with purity of heart or intention. After telling his followers that their virtuous lives must be the "salt of the earth" and the "light of the

---

[79] *To Autolycus,* Book I, nos. 2 and 7.

[80] *Commentary on the Sermon on the Mount,* I:8.

[81] Sermon 54:3.

world," he reminds them that their virtue must be "deeper than that of the Scribes and Pharisees." For instance, in the examples he uses of murder and adultery, he points out that true virtue goes deeper than external observance; that the evil is not merely in the external act but also in the intention or motive that inspires the act (anger, lust, etc.). These intentions have a moral quality even if one does not follow through with the act itself. St. Augustine makes two points about these examples. First, in speaking about the morality of the heart, Jesus does not abolish the old law which forbids killing, but completes it, as Jesus himself claimed (Matthew 5:17). Augustine notes: "He who teaches us not to be angry does not destroy the law that forbids us to kill. On the contrary, he implements it so that we may preserve our sinlessness outwardly so long as we do not kill, and safeguard it in the heart so long as we do not become angry."[82] Second, the morality of the heart does not have to do with spontaneous feelings but with deliberate intentions. Augustine distinguishes between one who "lusts after a woman" in the sense of a spontaneous "sensation of carnal pleasure" and one who, as Jesus put it, "looks at a woman to lust after her," that is, "with the aim and intention of lusting after her."[83]

Jesus, however, does not stop at pointing out the evil quality of the motives behind immoral behaviour. He goes on to say that even our noblest actions can be vitiated when they do not proceed from a "pure heart," when they are carried out from motives of self-interest. Again, examples are given. In this case Jesus refers to three types of "good works" (almsgiving, prayer and fasting) that have become for Christians traditional expressions of piety, especially as penitential practices during Lent. Hence the liturgy of Ash Wednesday includes these words of Jesus:

> "Be careful not to parade your good deeds before men to attract their notice; by doing this you will lose all reward from your Father in heaven. So when you give alms, do not have it

---

[82] *Commentary on the Sermon on the Mount*, I:21.

[83] *Commentary on the Sermon on the Mount*, I:33.

trumpeted before you; this is what the hypocrites do in the synagogues and in the streets to win men's admiration. I tell you solemnly, they have had their reward. But when you give alms, your left hand must not know what your right hand is doing; your almsgiving must be in secret, and your Father who knows all that is done in secret will reward you.

"And when you pray, do not imitate the hypocrites: they love to say their prayers standing up in the synagogues and at the street corners for people to see them. I tell you solemnly, they have had their reward. But when you pray, go to your private room and, when you have shut the door, pray to your Father who is in that secret place, and your Father who sees all that is done in secret will reward you.

"When you fast, do not put on a gloomy look as the hypocrites do: they pull long faces to let men know they are fasting. I tell you solemnly, they have had their reward. But when you fast, put oil on your head and wash your face, so that no one will know you are fasting except your Father who sees all that is done in secret; and your Father who sees all that is done in secret will reward you." (Matthew 6:1-6, 16-18)

Jesus makes two points about our good deeds, virtuous acts or acts of piety: (1) They should not be done for any kind of self-seeking motive, such as winning the praise and admiration of others or securing a reputation for holiness; (2) If we do act out of such motives of self-interest, we have already "received our reward" and can expect no other.

The first question about this passage that might occur to the reader of the Sermon on the Mount concerns the possible contradiction between these words of Jesus in which he says, "Be careful not to parade your good deeds before men" and a previous passage where he tells his followers that they are "the salt of the earth" and "the light of the world" and therefore their light "must shine in the sight of men" (Matthew 5:13-16). Which is it? Do we hide our virtue or put it on display? If we keep in mind that what is in question is not only external behaviour but also the disposition of the heart or intention behind the behaviour, there is no contradiction. What is condemned is not doing good deeds in the sight of others, but doing so with the *intention* of winning their praise and approval ("to attract their notice…for people to see them"). What is encouraged is not simply letting others see your good deeds but doing so in order that "they may give praise to your Father in heaven," when they see your goodness as a reflection of God's goodness. Even in the case of Jesus' good works, the typical response of the people was to praise God "for giving such power to men" (Matthew 9:8). Human praise may be the consequence or by-product of a truly well-lived life, but it is not what is directly sought by the pure of heart. The pure heart seeks only the good to be achieved. St. Augustine puts it this way: "Human praise ought not to be sought by the workers of righteousness. It ought to follow as a consequence of his righteous deeds."[84]

I believe that people generally show an intuitive awareness of the inappropriateness of seeking human praise for their good deeds by being genuinely embarrassed when they receive extravagant praise. How often have we seen truly generous and altruistic people deflect praise away from themselves? They will claim, for instance, that in their volunteer service to the sick, the disadvantaged or the handicapped they receive more than they give. By implication they are stating that to do such work in order to be praised and recognized would be an unworthy motive. It would in fact be hypocritical. Hence Jesus tells us not to act out of such self-seeking motives "as the hypocrites do." Such hypocrites are like "wolves in sheep's clothing" because they perform seemingly altruistic deeds with far from altruistic motives. This tends to give good works or "charity" a bad name, which in turn deters sincere and well-intentioned people from getting involved in worthy charitable projects. Hence Augustine tells us: "Sheep

---

[84] *Commentary on the Sermon on the Mount,* II:5.

are not to hate their own clothing, just because wolves often hide themselves beneath it."[85]

As we know, Jesus frequently charged the Pharisees with this kind of hypocrisy that pursued moral and religious rectitude not for the love of God but merely to win human praise, recognition and status (Matthew 23). It would be a mistake, however, for Christians to think that Jesus was being critical only of the members of a Jewish sect who were his contemporaries. The fact is that Pharisees and the religious attitude we call Pharisaism exist in all religions and in every historical period. There are Christian Pharisees whose moral and religious observance, if not aimed at winning human praise, is driven by an egocentric desire to prove themselves worthy and deserving of salvation – a salvation that can only be accepted in faith as a gift of God. St. Margaret of Cortona (13th century) claimed that Christ, in a vision, said to her: "More Pharisees crucify me today than at the time of my passion."[86]

When Jesus asks his followers to practice a kind of virtue that "goes deeper than that of the Scribes and Pharisees," he is talking not just about virtuous behaviour but about the purity of their hearts: their motives or intentions. The ideal is not just virtuous behaviour, but virtue that is free of egocentric motives such as the desire for human praise or the desire to impress God with one's virtue to win God's love and approval. This challenge gives rise to a second question about Jesus' teaching: Given human vanity and egoism, how is it possible to act out of such altruistic motivation that is free of any kind of self-interest? How is it possible, for instance, to do good for others (the extended meaning of "almsgiving") in a way that is free of any desire for recognition, gratitude or even a sense of personal satisfaction? Would I do a good deed for someone if I knew beforehand that he or she would not even acknowledge my efforts? I may not have my good deed "trumpeted" before me as in Jesus' example, but a bit of that same egoistic desire is nevertheless present in my behaviour.

The answer to this question, I believe, is twofold. First, it must be admitted that such self-transcending, altruistic, ego-less

---

[85] Commentary on the Sermon on the Mount, II:80.
[86] The Wisdom of the Saints, p. 161.

motivation is humanly impossible. Such a degree of self-forgetfulness is normally beyond human resources. Perhaps this is the very point Jesus wanted to make. As long as it is believed that the law of Christ and his gospel are a set of humanly observable rules, then the illusion persists that salvation is something that can be earned through one's human efforts. Jesus disabuses his followers of this idea by setting an ideal that is humanly impossible to fulfill. (Of course, there are those who stubbornly maintain the illusion by watering down Jesus' demands and thereby miss the point.) Salvation is not a human accomplishment; it is a gift of God's grace. Which brings us to the second part of our answer. While the goal of purity of heart or intention remains a humanly impossible ideal, the grace of God makes possible some partial realization or fulfillment of that ideal.

Now it is almost a cliché for Christians to say that this or that is possible "only through the grace of God." But what exactly does this mean? As noted in Chapter 6, the intended effect of faith – the trusting belief in God's unconditional love – is to liberate the believer from excessive self-preoccupation. Only this kind of inner transformation can make possible even a partial realization of Christ's call to purity of heart. Only when I am liberated from concern for myself can I be altruistically concerned about others. St. Gregory of Nyssa (fourth century) describes the transformation this way: "There is now a new birth, a new life, a new way of living, a transformation of our very nature."[87] Those of us who have ever said, "I feel like a new man/woman" after something as prosaic as a shower or a good night's sleep have no business calling this language extravagant.

Faith, therefore, is intended to bring about a personal transformation of the believer in which motives of self-interest (earning God's love and acceptance) give way to a more self-transcending, self-forgetful kind of motivation. Faith makes possible the freedom to strive for the good simply because it is the good and because it is in keeping with one's status as a child of God. One's moral and religious efforts are no longer burdened with the task of *earning* salvation. In other words, it frees believers from the tyranny of acting out of self-serving motives

---

[87] Sermon I.

183

and from the ulterior motive of always seeking their own advantage in the good they do for others. In short, it creates the possibility of purity of heart. By the same token, when our self-esteem is rooted in a divine and unconditional love that does not have to be earned, then we are liberated from the worrisome and anxious need to constantly prove ourselves and our worthiness. Consequently, there is that much less reason to bolster that self-esteem by seeking human praise, admiration and approval for our virtuous acts. And, again, our sense of integrity is heightened by the fact that our inner intention or disposition fits our external behaviour. To help someone in need is a virtuous act. To do so with a pure heart is to act for the good of the other person and not for any self-serving motive.

I believe that Jesus elaborates on this theme of purity of heart in the instructions he gives to his apostles when sending them out to preach and to bring to the people the message that "the kingdom of heaven is close at hand" (Matthew 10). In instructing them on how to conduct themselves, he tells them essentially to "keep it simple." They are to provide themselves with the minimum in the way of money and clothing and rely on the hospitality of those among whom they are labouring, "for the workman deserves his keep." There is one rather curious statement in these instructions, however, which seems to bear directly on the kind of inner dispositions or intentions they should have in carrying out their mission. Jesus tells the apostles: "If anyone does not welcome you or listen to what you have to say, as you walk out of the house or town *shake the dust from your feet.*" There is a way of understanding these words that makes it sound as if Jesus were suggesting a rejecting, belligerent, in-your-face attitude. ("Don't like what I have to say? Look, I'm shaking the dust of your crummy town from my feet!") Since, however, such advice seems contrary to Jesus' character, it is legitimate to look for another meaning. And even though Paul and Barnabas followed this advice literally (Acts 13:51), it is probably meaningful to most people today only in a metaphorical sense. Understood in this way, I believe these words have less to do with "getting even" and more to do with the question of how to handle failure. Surely this is what the apostles would experience when their message was met with indifference. In this case Jesus counsels them to put the experience behind them and move on to the next task. Shaking the dust from their feet might then be taken as symbolic of what would be referred to today as getting rid of "emotional baggage." Jesus' words might then be paraphrased as follows: "Don't hold on to the feelings of rejection, disappointment and frustration or they will drag you down and prevent you from effectively carrying out your next task." This seems possible, however, only to the extent that the work one does for others is carried out with a pure heart: solely for their benefit and welfare. Failure, rejection and indifference become problems precisely to the extent that one is driven by the self-serving intention of winning acceptance, approval, admiration, etc. Effective love and service of others require purity of heart or intention.

Now if we understand Jesus' advice to his apostles in this way, then it becomes clear that what he is counselling has a human, psychological value as well as a religious value. I would like to suggest that "purity of heart" is not restricted to doing everything purely "for the love of God." After all, Christians are taught that the love of God tends to be meaningless unless it translates into love of one's fellow human beings. If purity of heart refers to a kind of self-transcending motivation that is free of self-interest and self-seeking, then it refers to any good work that one does, whether religiously motivated or not. In short, it is both a religious and a human value: a sign of both religious and human maturity.

When seen as a sign of human maturity, there seems to be an analogy between what Jesus calls purity of heart and what psychologist Gordon Allport (1897–1967) referred to as the "functional autonomy of motives." An academic psychologist at Harvard University for almost his entire career, Allport was uncomfortable with both the psychoanalytic and the behaviourist accounts of human motivation. These were the dominant schools of psychological thought and therapeutic practice in Allport's time. Both implied that the adult subject was largely unaware of his or her true motives. The adult was still unconsciously driven by the instinctual drives or the social conditioning of childhood. Therefore, his or her consciously expressed motives could not be taken at face value. As Allport paraphrased this position, adult motives were seen as "conditioned, reinforced, sublimated or otherwise elaborated editions"[88] of innate drives or learned responses. My reactions to authority figures are determined by early parental conditioning, my choice of a marriage partner or career is determined by oedipal fixations, etc. In other words, my adult motivation is consistently an unconscious reaction to something in the past. This leaves little room for conscious goals, plans and intentions as dynamic motivators.

The whole thrust of Allport's theory of human personality was to acknowledge the dynamic motivational power of conscious, self-determining values, intentions and long-range goals. He would go on to describe the motivation of both the mature adult and the mature religious personality as "functionally autonomous," as independent of infantile and unconscious needs. To use one of Allport's favourite examples, suppose a young man chooses the same profession as his father (e.g., law, medicine, etc.). The young man's behaviour in emulating his father is not the same as his behaviour as a little boy when he imitated Daddy driving the car or going off to work in the morning. It might, however, satisfy the same infantile need to identify (or compete) with the father. This is what Allport would call the "functional continuity of motives," since the adult behaviour is continuous with or serves the same function as the childhood behaviour. This means that, at the level of motivation, there has been no real transformation in the passage from childhood to adulthood. Behaviour has changed but the motive behind the behaviour has not.

Allport insists, however, that "just as we learn new skills, so also we learn new motives."[89] It is possible that, while the young man may have originally been motivated by an infantile need to identify or compete with his father, he may, in pursuing his career, learn new motives. Now the profession is no longer a means of satisfying an infantile need but takes on a value of its own, becomes an end in itself and is pursued for its own sake. Allport believed that this is what usually happens in normal development. The motives of the mature adult become "functionally autonomous"; they do not serve the same purpose

---

[88] *Personality and Social Encounter* (Boston: Beacon Press, 1960), p. 96.

[89] Personality and Social Encounter, p. 149.

or function as one's infantile behaviour. The same criterion for maturity is then applied to the religious personality. What is true of human psychological maturity is true also of religious maturity; it is characterized by the functional autonomy of its motivation. What Allport calls the "religious sentiment" may be derivative: originally motivated by the need for comfort, security, companionship or the need for social status or conformity. The mature religious sentiment is one that has become independent of such needs and is free to direct itself to God and religious values directly; it does not have to serve the purpose of achieving some other human goal.

Even the mature religious sentiment, of course, may be a source of comfort, security, companionship, etc., but it is mature precisely to the degree that it has become an end in itself and not primarily a means of satisfying such human needs. Spiritual literature frequently refers to those times in one's life when this whole humanly comforting side of religion seems to be withdrawn from us. Invariably this is referred to as a time of "purification." It is primarily our motives that need to be purified. This is congruent with Allport's view that mature religion consists essentially in the maturity (or purity) of its motivation. Allport's view seems to be consistent with what Jesus has to say about purity of heart and also with what has been said about the transformation of motives that is the result of the Christian experience of grace and faith. The sense of freedom or liberation that seems to be a feature of religious experience might be interpreted psychologically as what Allport would call a liberation from "the magnet of self-centered motives." To be a mature religious person means that one is free to pursue God and religious values – to love God and one's neighbour – for their own sake, not to satisfy an infantile need for comfort and security or a narcissistic need for approval, reward or self-justification or a neurotic need to expiate guilt feelings. The process leading to both religious and human maturity is a process of leaning new motives.

Mature human beings pursue the conscious goals of life (work, family, human relationships, etc.) as an expression of their humanity and for the sake of the inherent good that these goals represent, not for the sake of satisfying some infantile, narcissistic need. Ideally, their behaviour is free of such ulterior motives. If they live and work well, others may praise and admire them. Although this may be a pleasant bonus or side effect of their efforts, it is not what they are directly seeking when they work hard at life's tasks or care for their loved ones. If this were so, they would not have the resources to pursue what is worth pursuing in the face of opposition and criticism. Their motives are "functionally autonomous." It is the same with Christians of mature faith. Their moral and religious efforts are free of ulterior motives. They do not try to love God and their neighbour for the sake of justifying themselves, proving themselves deserving of reward (human or divine). They do so, as we have seen, not to earn a reward from God but in response to a reward that God has already given. Their efforts are an expression of their identity as children of God. Freed from the necessity of earning salvation, they are able to love God and their neighbour for its own sake and not out of self-interest. In short, they can achieve a degree of "purity of heart."

If there is a neutral word that encompasses the meaning of both "functional autonomy of motives" and "purity of heart," it would perhaps be the word "simplicity." For some, this word has come to mean "simple-mindedness" at worst or "lacking sophistication" at best. In its original meaning, however, it refers to what is one or single in the sense of "unmixed." In our present context, simplicity refers to the singleness or unmixed quality of one's motives. We are told that one of God's attributes is his simplicity. This refers to the fact that God is one, not many; that God's goodness is unmixed with evil; that God's loving intentions towards us are free of ulterior or malign motives. Our human attempts to be Godlike in this respect translate into "integrity," which means to be one or whole. A person of integrity is the same person in all circumstances, a person whose external behaviour is consistent with internal feelings and intentions. As the saying goes, such people say what they mean and mean what they say. If our inner thoughts and intentions are at odds with our external behaviour, we are not one but divided, not simple but complex, not one person but two. The "simple" person is one whose motives are unmixed with ulterior, self-seeking motives.

To do good for others with simplicity would mean that one's intention is consistent with one's behaviour, that what is done is done with purity of heart. The loving deed proceeds from a truly loving disposition or intention that is free of self-interest. The service rendered, the encouragement offered or the act of kindness performed is done purely for the good of the other person. It is not done in order to win recognition, approval or praise, much less to earn one's salvation by "scoring points" with God. When one's motives have more to do with oneself than the other, this implied "put down" of the other is frequently all too obvious. Such ulterior motives create an incongruence or duplicity between the act and the intention. To be simple or pure of heart is to be like God. St. Vincent de Paul put it this way: "God in his nature is most simple and cannot admit of any duplicity. If we then would be conformable to him, we should try to become by virtue what he is by nature. We should be simple in our affections, intentions, actions and words; we should do what we find to do without artifice or guile, making our exterior conformable to our interior."[90] To perform an act that is outwardly generous and altruistic but to do so for motives of self-interest is to fall short of the ideal of human and Christian maturity.

This hallmark of maturity – whether we call it purity of heart or simplicity or functional autonomy of motives – is, in the Christian view, a prerequisite for "seeing God." Whether this refers to seeing God in eternity or, in some sense, in the here and now, this teaching implies that, even in his highest religious and moral endeavours, a person can be blinded to the vision of God by motives that are egocentric, self-seeking or self-absorbed. After Jesus warns his followers about the danger of fasting, praying and almsgiving for unworthy, self-seeking motives, he adds: "The lamp of the body is the eye. It follows that if your eye is sound, your whole body will be filled with light. But if your eye is diseased, your whole body will be all darkness. If then, the light inside you is darkness, what darkness that will be" (Matthew 6:22-23). In this passage there is an implied analogy between physical light and darkness and spiritual light and darkness. Hence, St. Augustine suggests: "In this passage we

---

[90] *The Wisdom of the Saints,* p. 179.

ought to understand the eye as the intention with which we perform all our actions."[91]

The intention or motive is the light within us making clear why we are doing what we do. If one's eye (one's intention) is diseased, then the light within turns to darkness. In this case the diseased "eye" is the flawed, self-seeking motive that creates a darkness in which God or even one's neighbour cannot be clearly seen. If one is completely self-absorbed, the vision of both God and one's neighbour is distorted. They cannot be seen for what they are but only as means towards one's own self-promotion and self-justification. Truly, then, one who lacks purity of heart cannot see God as he has revealed himself but sees only the distorted image of a God before whom one must constantly prove one's virtue. By the same token, one's fellow human beings, when seen merely as means of proving that virtue, are not seen for what and who they truly are, or even for what they really need. Even in this life purity of heart helps us to see both God and our neighbour as they were meant to be seen.

In the light of grace, of God's unconditional love, all self-seeking attempts to be recognized and rewarded for one's goodness have become pointless. God's love, like the love of a good parent, is given apart from any consideration of worthiness or deservedness. Christians are called to love one another in the same selfless and undemanding way: "You have received without charge, give without charge" (Matthew 10:8). In other words, you have been loved without having to earn it; love others in the same way. It is no longer necessary, therefore, to live in the darkness of self-interest and self-seeking motivation. As Jesus himself put it: "I, the light, have come into the world, so that whoever believes in me need not stay in the dark anymore" (John 12:46).

One could object, saying: Surely all of this is "much ado about nothing." Why is the loving intention so important? Is the "bottom line" not the good to be done – the homeless to be given shelter, the hungry to be fed, etc.? If, for instance, one's life work is in one of the so-called helping professions – teaching, nursing, social work, etc. – does it really matter whether one is motivated

---

[91] Commentary on the Sermon on the Mount, II:45.

by loving concern for others or by monetary gain as long as the job gets done efficiently? In the good that is done for others, does it matter whether one's feelings for them are loving, indifferent or even hostile as long as the good work is done? In trying to answer this question, the following three points should be kept in mind:

1. Christians are not called simply to do good deeds but to genuinely love one another. The Christian does not separate *doing* from *being*. We are called to be lovers, not just "do-gooders."

2. It is frequently the case that we are unable to genuinely love another person for whom we do good, either because we are preoccupied with our own personal problems or because of off-putting personality traits in the other. It seems to me that there are two ways of resolving this difficulty. First, we can use the time-honoured Christian cop-out and delude ourselves that we are fulfilling Christ's law of love by making the specious distinction between loving and liking. As if liking were some kind of optional extra added to love! (See Chapter 8.) Human parents certainly want their children to love one another. Can it be possible that God wants anything less for us? Moreover, Christians are called to love one another as God loves them. And how is that? The psalmist leaves us in no doubt: "The Lord takes *delight* in his people" (Psalm 149). Sounds like liking to me. The fact remains that it is impossible to love everyone in this way. There is, however, another way of resolving this difficulty without watering down Christ's law of love. That would be to do what is possible – to do good to those one finds impossible to love – but without deluding oneself that one is thereby fulfilling the Christian moral ideal of love. If I cannot love others, I still have to do what is needful for them. But I do so not with a sense of complacency, but with the humbling awareness that I am falling short of the ideal. There's nothing like an impossible ideal to keep one humble, but it is better to admit one's failure than to try to make that failure look like a success. At the same time, it is precisely this attitude of humble faith that makes it possible to see that a loving God accepts one's flawed efforts. God does not love us because we are perfect any more than we love others because they are perfect.

191

3. Are we really certain that the "bottom line" is the same whether we help others from egocentric or from altruistic motives? Is the same good accomplished? Or is it necessary to first love others in order to know what their deepest needs are? In other words, will I ever know what is truly best for someone else as long as I am preoccupied with myself and my own project of self-promotion? If I do not first love the other person with a love that is free of self-interest, I may well deprive that person of what he or she needs most – to be loved and respected and have his or her human dignity affirmed. It may be often or even usually impossible to achieve this kind of self-forgetfulness, but surely it would be foolish to contend that it makes no difference. The difference is the difference between vision and blindness; between clearly seeing another's needfulness and seeing only myself; between seeing the will of God and seeing only my own self-interest. Purity of heart leads to purity of vision.

On this final point, I suggest we give the last word to St. Cyril of Jerusalem: "Once the sun rises and spreads its light, a man dwelling in the dark sees clearly what he could not see before; so too the soul which receives the Spirit's gift is enlightened and sees the supra-human realities it previously did not know."[92] Surely this enlightenment applies to the way we regard others. If the "Spirit's gift" is the love that has been "poured into our hearts by the Holy Spirit" (Romans 5:5), then perhaps the enlightenment consists in being able, through love, to see the "supra-human" reality of the other, to see the other as God does. In this way we transcend the blindness that turns the other into a creation of our own projected fears, hostilities or prejudices.

---

[92] "On the Holy Spirit," Catechesis 16:16.

# 15. WHY ARE THE HUMBLE GREAT?

In one of his greatest moments of triumph – his entry into Jerusalem on Palm Sunday when everyone was proclaiming him as king and prophet – Jesus chose not to exalt himself. He chose to be a humble man riding a donkey and let others do the exalting. The evangelist interprets the event as fulfilling the prophecy of Zechariah: "Say to the daughter of Zion: Look, your king comes to you; he is humble, he rides on a donkey and on a colt, the foal of a beast of burden" (Zechariah 9:9). Lest anyone be tempted to think that the humility of Jesus was the pathological kind shown by those who make themselves passive doormats and mistake low self-esteem for humility, it is worth noting what happens when he enters the city. His first act is to drive the money changers and merchants – the commercializers of religion – from the temple. Sounds like the act of a very confident and self-assured man to me!

Humility is sometimes understood in a way that makes it the opposite of those very qualities valued by our culture – confidence, assertiveness, self-esteem, initiative and leadership. (If you lack any of these qualities, there are any number of self-help books or support groups that will help you acquire them.) True humility, of course, does not exclude any of these attributes. Everyone admires the confident, take-charge leader. He or she is admired even more if that strength of character is accompanied by self-effacing modesty and a self-deprecating sense of humour. Humility is all the more admirable in someone who seems to have so much to be proud of. This is the point of St. Paul's exhortation to the Philippians to imitate the humble attitude of Christ:

> In your minds you must be the same as Christ Jesus. His state was divine, yet he did not cling to his equality with God but emptied himself to assume the condition of a slave and became as men are; and being as all men are, he was humbler yet, even to accepting death, death on a cross. But God raised him high and gave him

the name which is above all other names so that all beings in the heavens, on earth and in the underworld should bend the knee at the name of Jesus and that every tongue should acclaim Jesus as Lord to the glory of God the Father. (Philippians 2:5-11)

In presenting Jesus Christ as the model of humility, St. Paul emphasizes these two points:

1. Humility does not involve a denial of one's intrinsic worth or human dignity. Jesus did not deny his divine status, he simply did not "cling" to it in a way that would interfere with his redemptive mission. A humble person is someone who does not let his or her ego get in the way of what is important in life. In an earlier chapter I suggested that Jesus' "emptying" of himself might be understood not as stripping himself of his divine attributes but as emptying himself of all human egoism and self-seeking. By transcending his ego in this way, he is able to focus entirely on the needs and concerns of others (a rather fundamental requirement for being a saviour!) and, in this way, reveal God's loving concern for humanity. In the same way, a humble person is one whose point of reference is not the self but the good to be achieved, the task to be completed, the other to be helped, etc.

2. Jesus' humility – the humble "emptying" of himself of egoistic self-seeking even to the point of dying on a cross as a criminal – resulted, paradoxically, in his glorification. He who "emptied himself to assume the condition of a slave" becomes one to whom every knee bows and whom every tongue acclaims as Lord. Jesus promises the same kind of paradoxical experience to his followers: "Anyone who exalts himself will be humbled, and anyone who humbles himself will be exalted" (Matthew 23:12). Our task is to try to understand this paradox. In what sense is the humble person "exalted"?

Christians might answer this question by pointing out that, despite their human limitations or humble life circumstances, they enjoy the exalted status of being identified with Christ as children of God and with Christ's mission to the world. Christians who serve Christ by helping him to achieve his purposes in the world see themselves as ennobled by this service, however humble a form it may take. It may not even be too fanciful, in this context, for them to compare themselves to the humble donkey who served Christ by carrying him into Jerusalem. In the difficult task of bringing Christ and his gospel into the world, Christians might even learn a thing or two from that donkey. St. Peter Claver, who dedicated his life to the care of the victims of the slave trade in 17th-century Latin America and who referred to himself as "the slave of the slaves," put it this way: "Every time I do not behave like a donkey, it is the worse for me. How does a donkey behave? If it is slandered, it keeps silent; if it is not fed, it keeps silent; if it is forgotten, it keeps silent; it never complains, however much it is beaten or ill-used, because it has a donkey's patience. That is how the servant of God must behave. I stand before you, Lord, like a donkey."[93]

And yet the donkey is ennobled by his humble service. In G.K. Chesterton's whimsical tribute, the donkey's description of himself shows that he is well aware of his ungainly appearance and lowly status:

> With monstrous head and sickening cry
> And ears like errant wings
> The devil's walking parody
> On all four-footed things.

Nevertheless, the donkey keeps silent when ridiculed or abused because he harbours a secret memory:

> Fools! For I also had my hour;
> One far fierce hour and sweet:
> There was a shout about my ears,
> And palms before my feet.

---

[93] *The Wisdom of the Saints,* p. 182.

Perhaps this is the secret of the truly humble. Their human dignity and self-esteem are rooted in something beyond and unaffected by human adulation and status.

Most people can identify with the donkey of Chesterton's poem. There are times when they feel, in one way or another, like a donkey – not much to look at or doggedly stubborn or incredibly stupid or not highly regarded by others or condemned to a humdrum existence in a dead-end job. When measuring our accomplishments by the standard of what our culture deems important or significant, it is easy to feel like an insignificant and unimportant donkey. In doing so, however, we can lose sight of our true inner worth. To be humble – with the kind of humility that Jesus enjoined – is to measure ourselves by a different standard. It is often said that "humility is truth." The anonymous author of *The Cloud of Unknowing* put it this way: "A man is humble when he stands in the truth with a knowledge and appreciation for himself as he really is."[94] St. Francis of Assisi puts a different slant on the notion of humility as truth: "What a man is before God, that he is and nothing more."[95] Francis' qualification is important. For Christians, the truth of humility is not just the truth about themselves as *they* see themselves, but the truth about themselves as *God* sees them. This truth is only known by seeing oneself through the eyes of faith.

And what does faith reveal about how God sees his children? Undoubtedly he sees them as sinners in need of forgiveness and redemption; as flawed human beings in need of healing; as sometimes thoughtless, self-serving egotists who frequently mess up their lives and their human relationships. This is the truth of faith that "humbles" the Christian. If this were the only truth the Christian possessed, humility might take the form of endless wallowing in a sense of worthlessness and guilt before a condemning God. Some readers might find here a description of what they like to call "Catholic guilt." And yet there is nothing Catholic or Christian about this kind of guilt. There is another side to the truth about oneself that faith imparts. Through faith Christians come to know themselves not

---

[94] *The Wisdom of the Saints*, p. 129.

[95] *The Wisdom of the Saints*, p. 130.

just as sinners, but as *redeemed* sinners; as people who, in spite of their broken and wounded state of sin, are loved by a God who reveals himself as a Father who would rather die as a convicted criminal than see his children live without hope. This is the truth that "exalts" the Christian. One is reminded of this twofold truth at every Mass that is celebrated. First comes the "penitential rite" – a public and collective acknowledgment of the community's fallen, sinful condition and its need for forgiveness and redemption. This is followed by the biblical readings announcing the "good news" of God's redeeming love and the memorial of Christ's redemptive death and resurrection in the Eucharist. The congregation's acknowledgment of their sinfulness is followed by the *celebration* of their status as *redeemed* sinners.

Nor can these two aspects of the revealed truth about the Christian's situation before God be separated. One is a precondition of the other. Only to the extent that Christians accept their sinfulness do they experience the "exalting" effect of God's grace. St. John Vianney put it this way: "Humility is like a pair of scales; the lower one side falls, the higher rises the other."[96] Or, as St. Vincent Ferrer puts it: "Christ, the master of humility, manifests his truth only to the humble and hides himself from the proud."[97] Both saints echo the words of Christ himself: "It is not the healthy that need the doctor, but the sick…. And indeed I did not come to call the virtuous, but sinners" (Matthew 9:12-13). Only the sick need a doctor, not the healthy. Only those who humbly acknowledge their need for redemption appreciate God's redeeming love. Only those who acknowledge the truth that humbles them before God can appreciate the truth that exalts them. Is this not true of human relationships as well? The more a person humbly recognizes that the love he or she receives from others is given freely and not earned or deserved, the more that love has the power to liberate and transform, to "exalt" that person. Ditto for the love of God. Unless it is humbly received as an undeserved gift, it loses the power to lift or exalt our spirit. Love that we believe we have "earned" or "deserve" is not very exalting. It is more likely taken for granted.

---

[96] *The Wisdom of the Saints,* p. 130.

[97] *The Wisdom of the Saints,* p. 129.

It is only this humble recognition of unworthiness that allows Christians to appreciate the eternal love with which they have been graced and their status as children of God. This is the truth that exalts them. But what of the other half of Christ's pronouncement: "Anyone who exalts himself will be humbled"? Here is the other side of the coin. One who exalts himself would seem to be one who tries to fashion his own status and self-worth on the basis of his own qualities and accomplishments. Such is the Christian who tries to fashion her own salvation by "good works" or a morally perfect life. Such a person never quite succeeds in silencing the voice of self-doubt and is burdened with the constant need to prove herself, whether to herself, to others or to God. In the end, such a person is humbled by the failure, self-doubt and anxiety that accompany this effort to exalt oneself. It is not difficult to imagine that it was to this kind of mentality that the prophet Joel addressed these words: "Let your hearts be broken, not your garments torn" (Joel 2:13). The breaking or tearing of the heart is the humble act of repentance. In this way one avoids the more serious kind of heartbreak that results from persisting in the self-righteous attempt to prove oneself and one's virtue. Commenting on these words of Joel, St. Jerome (fourth–fifth centuries) writes: "I bid you tear, not your garments, but your sinful hearts. Unless you tear them, they will, like swollen wineskins, break of their own accord."[98] The effort to manufacture one's own self-worth, status or importance is a heartbreaking task. For the person of faith, on the other hand, status and self-worth are not rooted in human ability and accomplishment, but are received in faith.

This is not just a religious truth but a human truth as well. In a very real sense, self-acceptance is built on the foundation of acceptance by others and status in one's own eyes is achieved only by being esteemed by another. Pride and humility, therefore, are not differentiated by one's degree of self-esteem, but by what one considers the source of that self-esteem. If the proud person tries to fashion his own self-worth through his own human resources, his efforts will always seem to fall short of this goal. No virtue or achievement will ever seem good enough. To the person of faith, human accomplishments are not

---

[98] "Commentary on Joel," *Patrologia Latina*, 25:967.

efforts to prove herself but a *response* to God, who has already affirmed her worth and status. Consequently, every accomplishment, no matter how small, is an acceptable part of that response. The humble are not only humble about what they are, but also about what they do. No gift is too small; no kind of work is insignificant; no act of kindness is too trivial. When we were children we gave our parents gifts of almost no material value, but our parents treasured them. Can God the Father act any differently towards his children?

Faith allows Christians to offer God whatever they are and whatever they do – great or small – with the assurance that God will accept it and do something with it. Consider the young boy who provided the loaves of bread and the fish for Christ to feed the multitude. What this boy offered was totally inadequate for the task at hand (feeding a huge crowd of people) but it was what he had, so he offered it and something wonderful happened. Now if what we believe about Jesus is true, he could have performed this miraculous feeding without the boy's contribution. The whole point of the story seems to be that, to carry out what he wants to do for the world, Christ wants (even needs?) human input, no matter how inadequate it may appear to be. Consequently, when confronted with the problems of our personal and collective life, it is not enough for us simply to sit back and wait for a miracle or to use prayer as a substitute for human effort. Jesus could not (or chose not to) work the miracle of the loaves and the fish without the loaves and the fish. Nor does he transform human life without human input. In the face of their human inadequacy, people who are humble realize how little they can do, but like the donkey and like the boy with the loaves and fish, they do it anyway and let God do the rest. All this can be dismissed as religious wishful thinking. And yet it is a common human experience to look back at the events in our lives and marvel at what we were able to accomplish or how we were able to survive difficult situations or overcome adversity. There is an attitude of humility in that old Christian rule of thumb: Work as if everything depended on you, pray as if everything depended on God. Humility is not passive; it is active. Humility means "do your thing" to the best of your ability, realizing that the outcome is not entirely in your hands.

Since it is necessary to humble oneself in order to be "exalted," the fullness of the Christian life, the liberating impact of being a child of God, can only be experienced by way of humility. This is why the Christian life begins with "repentance" – a humble recognition and acknowledgment of our inability to earn or be deserving of that status. In Catholic life, this act of repentance is constantly reaffirmed in two ways. First, as already noted, every celebration of Mass begins with the "penitential rite," the congregation's confession of sins and need for God's forgiving and redeeming grace. Second, every Catholic has the opportunity to express this act of repentance individually in the sacrament of reconciliation. This represents a uniquely Catholic way of humbling oneself in order to be exalted. It has probably not escaped the reader's notice that many (most?) Catholics have simply stopped "going to confession," as we used to call it, at least with any frequency. Why is this so? Does it point to a weakening of faith? Whatever reason is given, here is one that I think should not be overlooked. For generations of Catholics, there was a connection between confession and the Eucharist. Receiving the Eucharist was regularly preceded by the confession of sins. A "good" confession made one "worthy" to receive Communion. With the renewal of Vatican II, Catholics were disabused of the notion that confession was a necessary precondition for receiving the Eucharist. As sound as this advice was, for many Catholics it meant that the most compelling reason for confession was removed and they simply stopped confessing with any frequency. And yet I cannot avoid this impression: the Catholic mentality that linked the meaning of confession to the Eucharist demonstrated a valid intuition of faith, even though people may have been doing the right thing for the wrong reason. I suspect that what makes one truly "worthy" to participate in the Eucharist is not some kind of illusory freedom from sin but rather the humble acknowledgment of one's sinfulness. It is this act of repentance that reinforces one's faith and one's sense of solidarity with the Christian community. These are the true prerequisites for participation in the Eucharist. If the reader will forgive a rather lengthy digression, I believe that the thought of the great psychologist and psychotherapist Carl Jung (1875–1961) can help us to understand the relationship of confession to the

Eucharist and, at the same time, give us some insight into the meaning of humility as both a Christian and a human value.

In most psychological theories, the word "self" refers to the ego, the centre of one's uniqueness and individuality. The ego is the integrating and unifying centre of consciousness. To achieve "selfhood" (the goal of human growth) is to achieve this conscious awareness of one's uniqueness and individuality. Jung, however, believed that this was only part of the process of achieving selfhood. Beyond the development of conscious individuality lay the task of incorporating into consciousness the contents of the unconscious. It was necessary to actualize one's total personality, not just its conscious aspect. The ego is the centre of consciousness only. When unconscious contents are assimilated into consciousness, a new centre of personality emerges: Jung called it "the self." At the risk of oversimplifying, here is how Jung explains this process of growth. In infancy and early childhood, a conscious sense of self has not fully emerged. This conscious sense of individuality develops when I begin to make conscious differentiations. For instance, I begin by differentiating myself from others: "I am I, not you." This is the beginning of a sense of individuality and uniqueness. Further down the road, this self-awareness includes a sense of sexual identity: "I am a boy, not a girl" or vice versa. In normal development, consciousness will also eventually include a moral sense or conscience, based on the differentiation of good and evil.

This differentiation of opposites – self/others, male/female, good/evil – is the basis of consciousness. My conscious identity is formed by identifying, in each case, with one of the opposites. I am myself, not others; I am male, not female; I choose good, not evil. What happens now to the opposites with which I have not identified – that I have not made part of my conscious identity? They are relegated to the unconscious dimension of my personality. In this way they remain part of my total personality but not part of my conscious identity. As such, they act as a counterpart to and compensation for the one-sidedness of my conscious identity. Jung argues that, in order to become my whole and complete self, it is necessary to re-assimilate these unconscious aspects of myself and make them a part of my conscious identity. He refers to this process as rediscovering one's "soul." If a man, for instance, develops an excessively masculine or "macho" image and identity, then his repressed, unacknowledged "feminine" side is excluded from his conscious identity and relegated to the unconscious. This "contra-sexual" side that remains unconscious is what Jung called the "anima." In the case of the one-sidedly feminine woman, her unconscious masculine side is called the "animus." As Jung puts it, "A very feminine woman has a masculine soul, and a very masculine man has a feminine soul."

It may be easy enough to see how one's conscious sexual identity needs to be balanced with one's contra-sexual side. It also makes sense to say that one's sense of individuality (I am I, not others) needs to be balanced with a sense of identity and solidarity with other people. But how does all this apply to one's moral sense or conscience? To one's determination to pursue the good and reject evil? Is it necessary for the sake of wholeness and balance to assimilate or even surrender to the evil that the conscious mind (conscience) has rejected? Jung's answer would be no. At the same time, he would insist that, while it is a good thing to consciously *suppress* one's dark tendencies to evil (sin?), it is quite another thing to unconsciously *repress* those tendencies so that one remains unaware of them. It cannot be a good thing to remain unconscious of what Jung calls one's "shadow" or dark side, "the sum of all those unpleasant qualities we like to hide." Excluding one's capacity for evil and destructiveness from conscious awareness results in a lack of self-knowledge and a sense of identity that is an illusion. In the end, it does far more damage than the conscious acknowledgment of that dark side, since what is repressed creates tension and tends to find expression in primitive and destructive ways. The light of the morally upright image one presents to the world casts a shadow. Even from the human psychological perspective, it is better to consciously acknowledge that shadow than to repress awareness of it. Since the confession of sins involves such a conscious acknowledgment, it is not just meant to be a neurotic kind of "guilt trip." It is something that is meant to have a human as well as a religious value.

Psychologically, the repression of the shadow or dark side of personality has certain negative consequences. In the first place, this repression, like any kind of repression, creates tension because part of one's total self is denied expression. In other words, we pay for it because the longer and more deeply something is repressed, the more it tends to erupt and express itself in a negative and destructive way. It is as if the unconscious shadow wants to break through and compensate for the one-sidedness of the artificially created goodness of one's public image. Thus it happens that a highly rational, controlled and even-tempered persona could be the mask hiding dark moods, phobias and compulsions. In the same way, outstanding public virtue can exist side by side with private bad temper and irritability. This is simply the unacknowledged side of the person asserting itself. As Jung puts it: "A man cannot get rid of himself in favour of an artificial personality."[99] The person who is "too good to be true" is not an uncommon phenomenon. This description is usually applied to a person in whom something seems to be missing. We sense something stilted or artificial about such a person's goodness. We suspect that something not so nice is being repressed. It may also be true that this person is repressing something good. Jung suggests that, in repressing their dark, destructive impulses, such people may also be repressing their vital, instinctual, passionate energies, which are necessary for healthy living.

Repressing the shadow brings with it another negative consequence: it disrupts interpersonal and community life. What one represses is not recognized as part of the self. This repressed material tends to be unconsciously projected onto others. If I cannot bear to face my own undesirable traits, I find them in others. At all costs the source of evil must be located outside of myself. This is what Jesus referred to as finding the speck in another's eye while remaining blind to the beam in one's own eye (Matthew 7:1-5). This other who, through projection, has become the source of evil is now regarded as someone to be feared or against whom one must protect oneself (the usual targets being criminals, minorities, etc.). Herein lies one of the roots of bigotry and racism. In this way individuals isolate

---

[99] *Collected Works*, 7:307.

themselves from their fellow human beings. They see in others their own worst qualities, of which they are unconscious: their own shadow. In reference to this human tendency to repression and projection, Jung writes: "This principle is of such alarming general validity that everyone would do well, before railing at others, to sit down and consider very carefully whether the brick should not be thrown at his own head."[100]

What makes the dark side of personality so threatening that we refuse to recognize it? Jung would suggest that it is because the conscious self strives to be *perfect* rather than *whole* or *complete*. This implies that there is a way of pursuing moral perfection that is unhealthy, especially when it involves the repression of one's dark side. It goes without saying that "Christian perfection" can be pursued in this same unhealthy way. And it is precisely those who are "living under the law" – those who are trying to fashion their own salvation by impressing God with their virtuous lives – who have a vested interest in repressing their dark side. They cannot afford to become conscious of their moral failings, which they can see only as marks against them.

Jung suggests that while we are consciously pursuing the goal of perfection, the unconscious is pulling us towards the goal of wholeness or completeness. The first step towards that goal of wholeness is a healthy, conscious recognition of the shadow – what Christians call humility. From Jung's psychological perspective, recognizing one's dark side leads to genuine self-acceptance. This he considers to be "the essence of the moral problem and the epitome of a whole outlook on life." Jung continues:

> That I feed the hungry, that I forgive an insult, that I love my enemy in the name of Christ – all these are undoubtedly great virtues. What I do to the least of my brethren, that I do unto Christ. But what if I should discover that the least amongst them all, the poorest of all the beggars, the most impudent of all the offenders, the very enemy himself – that these are within

---

[100] *Collected Works*, 10:39.

me, and that I myself stand in need of the alms of my own kindness – that I myself am the enemy who must be loved – what then? As a rule, the Christian attitude is then reversed; there is no longer any question of love or long-suffering; we say to the brother within us "Raca" and condemn and rage against ourselves.[101]

To recognize one's shadow is to discover oneself as "the enemy who must be loved." For Jung this is the most difficult moral task one faces – to accept, love and forgive oneself, dark side and all. It is easier to love and forgive the enemy outside of ourselves and remain unconscious of our own need for forgiveness. Self-acceptance is difficult because it requires us to accept our total self, including those aspects we prefer to ignore. I believe that Jung's words remind us of something very important about the sacrament of reconciliation that is sometimes too easily forgotten: that it is supposed to lead the penitent to self-acceptance, not self-rejection; that it is intended to reconcile the penitent not only with God but with himself or herself. For the Christian, this act of self-acceptance becomes possible in the light of divine forgiveness and acceptance. In fact, the divine acceptance implied in the word "grace" cannot be received in faith unless it is understood as acceptance of one's *total* self – dark side and all. Only by humbly recognizing our dark side in this way can we be "exalted" by the grace of God.

When I suggest that, in their use of the sacrament of reconciliation, Catholics may often have been doing the right thing for the wrong reason, I mean to say that there is a way of using the sacrament to pursue moral perfection that amounts to an attempt to, as Jung would say, "get rid of oneself in favour of an artificial personality." Perhaps the requirement of a "firm purpose of amendment" deluded penitents into believing that, by force of willpower, they could eliminate the dark side of their personality and conform to a conscious ideal image of themselves that excludes that dark side. Of course Christians

---

[101] "Psychotherapists or Clergy" in *Modern Man in Search of a Soul* (New York: Harcourt, Brace and World, 1933), p. 235.

must always try to overcome bad habits and character traits and conform their lives to the image of Christ. But there is more to confession than an exercise in self-improvement. It is easy to forget that confession is primarily about *forgiveness*. It is a renewal of the penitent's faith in the fact that God forgives and accepts him or her in spite of these flawed efforts at self-improvement. When we keep this in mind, it is not necessary to disown our dark side, since it too is part of our total self that God loves and accepts. The dark, negative side of the self is equivalent to the condition of sin or egoism that St. Paul discovered he could not rid himself of, but only submit to God's forgiving grace (Romans 7). The fact that we will always need this divine forgiveness is the kind of self-knowledge that should be one of the fruits of confession. It is also the kind of self-knowledge that is blocked by the illusion that we can achieve a degree of moral perfection that "merits" God's acceptance.

Catholics are sometimes criticized for going to confession and then committing the same sins all over again. It seems to me that the only answer to such criticism is: Of course they do. Confession is not spiritual or moral "dry cleaning." It is not an attempt to disown oneself, to get rid of all those negative traits that make up one's dark side. The penitent does not strike a bargain with God, begging for forgiveness on condition of shaping up and "doing better." The penitent's attitude is not, "If only I can do better, then God will forgive and accept me." It is rather, "God loves and accepts me just as I am. Therefore I should try to do better." Confession or reconciliation is meant to be a renewal of the penitent's faith in the divine forgiveness given once and for all in Christ by a God who loves and accepts all his children, warts and all. In the light of that forgiveness, the penitent is able to accept and forgive himself or herself, even the dark side. Only by accepting and not rejecting it does he or she gain some control over that side. Jesus himself told his followers, "Come to terms with your opponent in good time" (Matthew 5:25). I suspect he meant the opponent within as well as the opponent without.

If the recognition of the shadow – or what Christians would call repentance – is necessary for personal transformation or wholeness, it is equally essential for the building up of the

Christian community. As previously noted, the repression of the shadow leads to projection of evil onto others, turning them into objects of fear, suspicion or hostility. This obviously creates a barrier between self and others and, therefore, a barrier to genuine community. But when one recognizes that the evil of the world also resides within oneself, then such defensive projections are withdrawn. The result is that the need to relate to others from a position of superiority or defensiveness can also be given up. One can now relate to others as equals. Isolation is transcended and community becomes possible. There is no such thing as "instant community"; it doesn't happen just because people say, "Let's all love one another." It can only be achieved by entering through the "narrow gate" of repentance, the humble acknowledgment of sin and guilt (the shadow), through humility. The traditional Christian understanding is that the bond that unites the Christian community is the realization that it is a community of sinners. Whenever this community gathers to celebrate the Eucharist, it recognizes this fact by beginning with the penitential rite, the confession of sin. Each individual Christian's personal act of repentance is the precondition for participation in that community and in its communal act of worship. Catholics, therefore, were not entirely off the mark in linking the sacrament of reconciliation to the Eucharist. It is not freedom from sin, however, but the recognition of their sinfulness that makes them "worthy" to receive the Eucharist.

From both the human and Christian point of view, then, to humble oneself is to be exalted. Through the humble recognition of our lack of moral self-sufficiency, our otherwise isolated ego is exalted to a condition of greater wholeness or completeness as well as a greater sense of participation in community. In both cases, the isolated ego grows by becoming part of a greater reality. We would be hard-pressed to find a better description of religious experience. *The Globe and Mail* of August 31, 2000, carried a picture of the folksinger Victoria Williams. The accompanying caption describes her singing in these words: "Her kind of exaltation is rooted in humility." And so is everyone's.

# EPILOGUE: Some Reminders and Rules for Survival

The central theme of this book may be stated this way: The Christian message is a message of grace that can only be received in faith. Reduced to its simplest terms, this means that, in the person of Jesus Christ, God has proclaimed his unconditional love for all human beings. This in turn means that God's love and acceptance and whatever reward God promises cannot be earned or deserved. We can respond to God's "I love you" – like anyone's –with trusting belief, or reject it. These are the only alternatives. To insist on a third option – "earning" that love – is an insult to the lover. As we know from human experience, love – unlike respect, admiration, etc. – either happens or does not happen; it cannot be made to happen through our human efforts. The "good news" of the Christian message is that the divine love and acceptance has happened and we can respond to that happening only with a yes or a no. All our efforts to please God and live a good life are a *response* to that freely given love (grace) and an expression of that trusting belief (faith).

So strongly did St. Paul feel about the inadequacy of human effort to earn salvation that he wrote to the Philippians:

> I have accepted the loss of everything, and I look on everything as so much rubbish if only I can have Christ and be given a place in him. I am no longer trying for perfection by my own efforts, the perfection that comes from the law, but I want only the perfection that comes through faith in Christ, and is from God and based on faith. (Philippians 3:8-9)

St. Augustine echoes this sentiment: "God gave a law requiring uprightness of men who were not upright in order to bring home to them their sinfulness, not to take it away. The only thing that takes away sin is the gift of that faith which finds expression in love."[102] There is nothing wrong with trying to observe God's law; it only becomes "rubbish" when it is used as currency to "pay" for salvation. Salvation is a gift that can only be received in faith – a faith that makes love possible.

This, in a nutshell, is the point that has been expressed over and over again in this book. To justify this repetition, the author can only argue that it is a point that needs to be repeated frequently for the following reasons: (1) This book is primarily an attempt to assist Catholics in their quest for a distortion-free understanding of their faith. At the same time, it is based on the conviction that neglect or misunderstanding of this fundamental truth is the most widespread distortion of the faith among Catholics. It has had an uneven history even among Protestants, despite the fact that the Reformation was, more than anything else, an attempt to reaffirm the truth that salvation came through grace and faith and not through "good works." (2) When the meaning of the terms "grace" and "faith" is distorted, everything else gets distorted. Morality becomes a legalistic, anxiety-ridden attempt to earn God's love, God becomes a lawgiver, and the Church becomes his law-enforcement agency. (3) When the meaning of salvation through grace and faith (God's love and one's belief in it) is truly appreciated, this throws light on the meaning of all other aspects of the Christian life. In the light of the Christian message of grace the following ideas become clear:

(i) God can be seen as a loving Father who loves his children before and apart from anything they do to deserve that love;

(ii) Salvation, therefore, is not something to be earned, but a gift received in faith;

(iii) The moral life of the Christian is not an attempt to earn something from God but a response to what has already been given. This does not rule out serious moral effort; it just takes the anxiety out of it;

---

[102] "Preface to Commentary on Galatians," *Patrologia Latina,* 35:2106.

(iv) Sacraments are not *duties* performed to earn one's salvation. They are *celebrations* of a salvation accomplished once and for all in Christ;

(v) The Church is not just some kind of ecclesiastical bureaucracy responsible for preserving faith and morals. It is all of us – religious and laity – united in a community of faith, the community that results from a shared faith and ideally the kind of love that faith makes possible;

(vi) Where faith is genuine, the believer does not need to justify or prove himself or herself to be deserving of salvation. This makes possible a kind of self-forgetfulness, which in turn makes possible some partial fulfillment of the Christian moral ideal and the Christian way of life. When Christians are free of concern about themselves and their salvation, they are able to love and be concerned about others in a more selfless way. When our sense of self-worth or self-esteem is rooted in the divine love and acceptance, we can be poor in spirit since there is no need to find it in material possessions; we can be pure of heart since there is no need to find it in the praise and approval of others; we can be humble since there is no need to find it in an image of blameless personal perfection.

To see God as our loving Father and to have a confident faith in that Father's freely given love (grace) is, to my mind, a key to making sense out of many other aspects of Catholic teaching. It is also a way of "keeping it simple." The complicated stuff should be left to theologians – they seem to enjoy it. The Christian message is for everyone and I don't think God intended to confuse anyone. But simple does not mean shallow; it means focusing on what is most important, basic and fundamental. Perplexed Catholics can move beyond perplexity by focusing and by keeping it simple. Still, being a Catholic means being part of the Catholic community, dealing with the difficulties, conflicts and issues that afflict and sometimes divide that community. At the risk of being presumptuous, I humbly offer the following "rules for survival."

# TEN RULES FOR SURVIVAL FOR CATHOLICS

**1. Don't put limits on God's love.** As a Catholic you are unfortunately saddled with expressions like "the one true Church" and "papal infallibility" – heavy burdens indeed! These clumsy expressions of legitimate claims cannot simply be erased; they are part of Catholic history. What you can do is to interpret them in a way that emphasizes the fact that God's healing, saving, life-giving grace is intended for everyone, everywhere. There is only one "chosen people of God" and it includes everybody.

**2. Let God be God.** You are free to refer to God as "he" or "she" as long as you remember that God is a mystery beyond all categories, including gender. Don't lose sight of the grandeur and the mystery for the sake of winning a gender battle. Above all, do not reduce God to an impersonal "it" (life-force, energy, etc.). This may make you feel intellectually sophisticated, but no "it" ever died on a cross for anyone.

**3. Let God be a father.** Remember that God the Father is at least as good a parent as you are or the parents you know are. This means that, no matter how badly you mess up, God remains on your side. When you confess your sins (in or out of the sacrament of reconciliation) you are reminding yourself of that fact. And you're getting some help and encouragement to clean up the mess. Isn't this what good fathers do?

**4. Develop a faith-inspired skepticism.** Do not simply equate "what the Church teaches" with what you read or hear in the media, what your friends and co-workers say, or even what you hear from the pulpit or in the classroom. (Or, for that matter, what you read in this book!) Perplexed Catholics are often that way because they have – whether through their own fault or that of their pastors and teachers – a distorted understanding of what the Church really teaches or expects of them.

**5. Be responsible for your own faith.** Do not assume that you can operate as an adult Christian with the understanding of the faith you had when you graduated from your Catholic elementary school. Would you try to meet the challenges of adult life with a Grade 8 understanding of what it takes to be a husband/wife, parent or informed member of society? An inadequate understanding of the faith is not always someone else's fault. At the end of the day, we are each responsible for our own religious immaturity. Until a misguided translator substituted the words "We believe" at the beginning of the Nicene Creed, there were only two places in the liturgy of the Mass where the first person singular was used: the *Confiteor* ("I confess") and the *Credo* ("I believe"). Even when gathered as a community, there are two things for which we take personal responsibility – our sins and our faith. It is ultimately *my* responsibility to at least try to get it right.

**6. Be responsible for your Church.** The phrase *Ecclesia semper reformanda* has long been an integral part of Catholic tradition. It simply means that the Church always stands in need of reform. This is so obvious that in today's jargon it would be called a "no brainer." But is this axiom not true of all institutions run by human beings? At least the Church explicitly acknowledges it. Catholic tradition also speaks of the *sensus fidelium*. This phrase is difficult to translate literally, but it implies that the faithful, that is, the laity, have a "sense" or intuitive understanding of what is true in the area of doctrine and morals. It further implies that, in formulating doctrine, the pope and the bishops listen to and, to some extent, reflect the laity's understanding of doctrine. All of this suggests to me that the laity have some responsibility for what goes on in the Church and for the reform and renewal of the Church. Remember that, as a baptized Catholic, you have certain rights. These include the right to meaningful liturgies, homilies that encourage your faith and adequate instruction in the faith. If you are not getting these, you're allowed to ask why not.

7. **Appreciate your freedom.** Remember that, as a child of God, you have a personal relationship with God that no one can deprive you of or interfere with. This relationship is the basis for the freedom "with which Christ has made us free." But remember also that freedom is for those who are willing to assume the responsibility that goes with freedom. Accordingly, when the Church teaches that one should "always obey the certain judgment of his conscience," these words should be taken seriously and acted upon. At the same time, it should be recognized that, if freedom of conscience implies a moral stance that goes beyond blind obedience to Church teaching, it also implies a responsibility that makes one ultimately answerable to God.

8. **Be critical, not self-righteous.** Don't let constructive criticism of the Church degenerate into self-righteousness. It has been observed that, if the Church were suddenly everything they wanted it to be, some Catholics would have no further reason to belong to it. Why? Because they would no longer have an outlet for their need to be "injustice seekers" and to feel superior. Their criticism does not proceed from concern for the Church but from self-interest and psychological need. It is entirely appropriate and indeed an obligation to speak out – even with outrage – at the failings of the Church and its members. At the same time, it is sobering to recall that the Church is a "community of sinners" and if you don't recognize yourself as one of the sinners you will not feel at home in this community, nor will your criticism be balanced with compassion.

9. **Remember that doubt is not a sin.** Doubt is an integral part of faith. This will be easier to remember if you keep in mind that faith means more than belief in doctrines. It also means trusting God's declaration of love and acceptance. Faith in another's love is a fragile possession. The statement "God loves me" is sometimes more difficult to believe than a statement like "the Holy Spirit proceeds from the Father and the Son" – especially at times when you find it difficult to love yourself.

**10. Be true to yourself.** Don't put the cart before the horse or get the order of things backwards. To repeat our basic premise one last time, the Christian life is not an effort to earn something from God; it is a response to what God has already given you. The more fundamental moral question is not "What must I do?"; it is "What has been done for me?" You don't go to Mass to win God's approval or acceptance; you go to celebrate the fact that you are already accepted. You don't go to confession to earn God's forgiveness; you do so to experience, through human voice and gesture, the forgiveness that is always yours. You don't live a good life in order to become a child of God; you do so because you already are a child of God. The Christian life is not so much about striving to become something you are not, it is about being true to what you already are. In other words, it is a matter of integrity.

\* \* \* \* \*

What is most tragic about the religious experience of many Catholics is that they are unable to enjoy their religion. Perhaps this is their own fault; perhaps it is due to factors that have nothing to do with religion. Many perplexed Catholics may find it impossible to "enjoy religion," especially if their experience of Catholicism has left them confused, angry or guilt-ridden. I would suggest that most of those Catholics who remain in the Church do so because they have looked beyond the sources of anger and confusion and discovered a tradition that they want to be part of: a storehouse of moral teaching, spirituality and ritual that gives depth and meaning to life and a worldwide community of believers who share a conviction about the essential goodness of the human and natural world. In short, they have discovered the well-kept secret that being Catholic is *fun*. As usual, Andrew Greeley has put it best:

> It is fun to belong to something, it is fun to
> believe that God is close to us, loving us like a
> spouse, a parent, a friend. That's why Catholics
> stick to their church, come what may. That's
> why the confusion and the chaos in the church

in the years since the end of the Second Vatican Council has not driven Catholics out of the church despite all the attempts of us priests and bishops to drive them out! Despite the creeps and party-poopers, the puritans and the spoil-sports, the kill-joys and parade ruiners, Catholicism is too much fun to leave.[103]

Some may accuse Greeley of wearing rose-coloured glasses. But perhaps our distorted understanding of the faith is largely due to taking "the creeps and the party-poopers, the puritans and the spoil-sports, the kill-joys and the parade ruiners" far too seriously.

---

[103] "It's Fun to Be Catholic", in Michael Leach and Therese, J. Bouchard (Eds.). *I Like Being Catholic* (New York: Doubleday, 2000).

# GLOSSARY

The purpose of this book is to make sense of some of the language of the Catholic tradition by relating that language to our human experience. The following is a thumbnail review of the main terms we have encountered.

## Church

The Church is meant to be both a visible institution and a community of faith and love. The Church exists because the ultimate purpose of the individual experience of grace and faith is to render us capable of love and thereby create community. The full realization of faith is community, and the full realization of that community will be the kingdom of God. As with our human growth, our growth as members of the Church is a transition from dependency on the Church as a nurturing mother figure to free and responsible membership in the community of faith.

## Eternal Life

Though the nature of eternal life as promised in the Christian message is ultimately a mystery, we know that it will be the completion and perfection of the life of faith that we are now living. Hence we can hazard the following statements: (1) The life of eternity begins here and now with the experience of grace and faith and the transformation that experience brings about. This is the beginning of the "new creation." Eternal life does not begin only with physical death. (2) Both human life and the life of faith are essentially communal. Genuine life is always experienced in conjunction with another or others. Eternal life, then, must have this same quality. It is not merely the final reward of an individual life but the completion and perfection of a community.

## Faith

Faith is the human response to the revelation of God's grace, God's unconditional love. It is our total response to that love. It therefore includes not only intellectual assent to doctrines about God (belief), but also trust in God's declaration of love and a moral commitment to live as children of God who wants to be our father. Trusting belief in God's freely given love liberates us from the need to earn that love through strict observance of the moral law. This "freedom from the law" does not mean ignoring the law but being free to observe it from a different motive – as a response to a love already received rather than as an attempt to earn that love. It also means that, since we are no longer under pressure to "prove ourselves," we are also liberated from the self-preoccupation that goes with living "under the law." This freedom from self is the precondition for genuinely loving others. Hence the vital connection between faith and love in both our human and religious lives.

## God

The question of the existence of God is more a philosophical question than a religious one. By the same token, rational arguments for the existence of God are not the foundation of our faith. Faith runs deeper than reason. Moreover, these arguments prove only the existence of a "supreme being," and God is not merely the supreme being but the "ground of all being" or "being itself." Since God is not "a being," he can only be known through metaphors and images (including the image of "supreme being"). The Christian image of God as "Father" is a revealed image that represents the way God wants to be known to us. As such it tells us something about God but not the whole truth about God. As we know from human experience, the term "father" does not exclude motherly qualities. Hence our tradition contains "compensatory images" ("mother Church" and "mother Mary") to express the "feminine" side of God.

# Grace

Christians believe that the healing of separation (sin), that is, salvation, is brought about by the grace of God. To avoid any "magical" understanding of that word, it is best to think of the grace of God as the love of God as revealed in the person of Christ, with emphasis on the fact that this love is freely given and does not have to be earned. This is the essence of the Christian message. The legalistic attitude that acts as if God's love and acceptance have to be earned by religious and moral observance is a distortion of that message. The love of God is like human love in at least this respect: it cannot be earned.

# Jesus Christ

Questions about the nature of Jesus (human or divine?) are less important than the question of the meaning of Jesus for our lives: How does Jesus bring about our salvation and reconciliation with God (atonement)? The understanding of Jesus as the revelation or human expression of God's love for us seems to incorporate other "theories of atonement." The love that Christ reveals is liberating (ransom theory), forgiving (satisfaction theory), and transforming (moral influence theory).

# Morality

The moral life of the Christian is rooted in the experience of grace and faith in the following ways: (1) Our moral effort is a response to grace (love) already received, not an attempt to earn that grace; (2) The experience of living under grace liberates us from the self-absorption of living under the law and enables us to fulfill, at least partially, the Christian moral ideal of selfless love; (3) The experience of grace and faith creates a personal relationship between God and us (we become children of God). Fidelity to that relationship is the ultimate criterion for making moral decisions. Moral laws are guidelines to help us remain faithful to that relationship: to live as children of God.

## Religion

According to one derivation, the word "religion" is from the Latin *religare,* which means to bind together again. The function of religion is to bind together or make whole again what has been fragmented or separated. Religion, therefore, aims to heal the state of separation (sin) that characterizes human existence. In religious language, this healing of separation or making whole again is called "salvation."

## Sacraments

Catholics believe that the seven sacraments are "effective signs of grace." They are visible signs that make the grace or love of God present. In this way they continue the redemptive work of Christ. The seven sacraments reflect the incarnational, sacramental nature of Catholicism which maintains that the God who revealed himself in a flesh-and-blood human being continues to reveal himself through the human and natural world. The material world is a "sacrament" – a visible sign – of God's presence. God is encountered not just through words but through the senses as well.

## Sin

Understood not as a transgression of the moral law but as a state in which we live ("original sin"), sin is an aspect of the human condition. It is the state of separation from oneself, from others and from what is ultimate and infinite (God). This state of separation is part of human existence. It represents a "fallen" condition because it limits human existence and separates us from the fullness of life that we desire and were meant to live.

## Spirituality

The desire to heal the various forms of human separation is not an exclusively religious desire. It is a basic human desire. Since this desire can be expressed in either religious or non-religious ways, it is best to refer to it as a spiritual desire. In the same way, the values we pursue in order to satisfy that desire (wholeness, community and ultimacy) can be regarded as both religious and human values – as spiritual values.

**AGMV** Marquis

MEMBER OF SCABRINI MEDIA

Quebec, Canada
2001